The Complete
Personality
Assessment

The Complete Personality Assessment

Psychometric tests to reveal your full potential

Jim Barrett and Hugh Green

KoganPage
LONDON PHILADELPHIA NEW DELHI

First published in Great Britain and the United States in 2011 by Kogan Page Limited

120 Pentonville Road	1518 Walnut Street, Suite 1100	4737/23 Ansari Road
London N1 9JN	Philadelphia PA 19102	Daryaganj
United Kingdom	USA	New Delhi 110002
www.koganpage.com		India

© Jim Barrett and Hugh Green, 2011

The right of Jim Barrett and Hugh Green to be identified as the author of this work has been asserted by them in accordance with the Copyright, Designs and Patents Act 1988.

ISBN   978 0 7494 6373 1
E-ISBN   978 0 7494 6374 8

British Library Cataloguing-in-Publication Data

A CIP record for this book is available from the British Library.

Library of Congress Cataloging-in-Publication Data

Barrett, Jim.
    The complete personality assessment : psychometric tests to reveal your true potential / Jim Barrett, Hugh Green.
        p. cm.
    Includes bibliographical references.
        ISBN 978-0-7494-6373-1 – ISBN 978-0-7494-6374-8   1. Personality tests.
2. Personality assessment.   I. Green, Hugh, 1941-   II. Title.
        BF698.5.B39 2011
        155.2′83–dc22

                                                                                                    2011013894

Typeset by Graphicraft Ltd, Hong Kong
Printed and bound in India by Replika Press Pvt Ltd

Contents

Introduction

'Treat someone as [the person] he wants to be and he will become that person.'

Johan Wolfgang von Goethe (1749–1832)

After Goethe, with the benefits of modern psychological techniques, we are able to say:

'Treat yourself as the person you want to be and you will become that person.'

Jim Barrett and Hugh Green

This book aims to tell you the truth. We consider this is the best a friend can do. The truth gives you the only means of enabling you to find out who you are. Being told the truth and telling yourself the truth are essential if you are to take responsibility for yourself. No one else is in a better position to make choices about your life.

People know who you are, although you may not think they do. People know more about who you are than you think. You know more about them than they think you do. There is more to you than people think they know. There is more about who you are than you know yourself.

By the character you have been, you are recognized as who you are. If you do something different from what people expect, they say, 'That's not like you!' Sometimes you behave in ways that you do not expect, and say, 'That's not like me!' Sometimes you hate yourself for repressing yourself and not doing something you know you want to do.

Of course, all your behaviour is you, but, as with every other human being, most lies beneath the surface. What lies there, and what is there that you can make use of, is what this book will help you reveal.

The best estimate of science is that each one of us has a potential that we are born with, our genes determining the person we shall be. But the crucial thing is that how we shape our lives for ourselves is within the domain of our choosing. That we can do whatever we choose sounds simple enough, but this is where the problems start. It is because we frequently think we have no choice or that, even if we do have a choice, we are afraid to make it.

It is paradoxical that, when we know that we can choose to do something that has the potential to make us feel good about ourselves, we often shrink from doing it. So often, there are inhibitions that we allow to put restraints upon ourselves. Fear of the outcome makes us check our actions. Although we have a vision for ourselves, the gap between here and there seems so wide, and the risk of failure, humiliation or rejection so strong. It sometimes seems better to compromise, to tell ourselves that what we imagine for ourselves is just an idle dream – it is not us. So we make excuses and deceive ourselves by pretending that we have no choice. The consequence is that people never know who we really are. Even worse – we never know who we really are! Sadly, we live with a bitter sense of underachievement, of never having been fully alive and of never having been ourselves.

This book uses well-researched psychometric and analytical techniques to help you assess who you really are. It deliberately invites you to examine possible areas of discrepancy or imbalance in your life. It takes a structured approach to assist you understand how underlying emotions work in order to enable you to control them for your benefit. Ultimately, the aim of this book is to enable you to actualize the person you are.

Synopsis

The questionnaires in this book are designed so that you can obtain feedback and complementary views from key people around you, if you choose.

Chapter 1: your personality

The six-factor personality test reveals six critical characteristics that describe your own individual 'style'. The results enable you to better understand your disposition as well as that of others. Applying this knowledge effectively is a certain way of staying on the road to personal and professional success.

Chapter 2: your behaviour and attitude towards work

The career development profile investigates how motivated you are by different types of work and also how you approach situations at work. Areas of uncertainty and conflict are highlighted in order to assist you to carry out the most suitable career planning. There are practical exercises to guide and assist you in pursuing your choices.

Chapter 3: your work, life and well-being

The life balance profile helps you to critically assess key areas of your life associated with contentment and success. The relative balances in your life are essential if you are truly to experience living to your full potential. Depending upon the results, you are asked to examine where and in what ways you may be holding yourself back. Suggestions are provided as to how to overcome these so that you really can achieve what you want in order to make balanced life choices.

CHAPTER 1

Who are you?

In this chapter you can complete the six-factor personality test, which reveals vital characteristics about your style, your behaviour and your relationships. The analysis of your results will raise your awareness of yourself and your potential. How you may have been, perhaps unknowingly, under-fulfilling yourself is explained, and numerous exercises will show how you can enable yourself by developing the insights you have gained.

Are you content with who you are?

The 'real you' is, very possibly, not the person you appear to be! It is the person you could be.

Although you have characteristic behaviours by which others recognize you, there are many aspects of you that you may not express. Perhaps you are unsure how to or perhaps you have qualities of which you are not even aware. These aspects may be lying dormant, latent within you. You may get only occasional glimpses of them when you are put into an unusual situation that demands that you stretch your talents or, more usually, in your imagination, where they fleetingly reveal themselves to beckon you to be the 'real you'.

On the premise that the 'real you' is, actually, likely to be different from the person that we see today, we will find it useful to establish if there are developments that you want to make. The gap that arises between how you are now and your real self is what is often termed 'potential'. Being anything else than the person who uses his or her potential will make you feel limited. Therefore this section will also establish a basis upon which you can take an objective approach to overcoming any limiting factors you think there may be, with a view to the development of your personality in the ways you want.

Six-factor personality test

Part 1: How I am

In this questionnaire, be honest about how you now see yourself. It is about how you are at this time in your life. It is not about how you imagine you could be or would like to be. Take a good, hard look at yourself; it is especially important to be honest even if there are things you do not like so much and even if you would like to be different. The results are for you and, the more honest your answers, the clearer the picture, and the more benefit you will get from the later exercises.

You have to say whether you agree or disagree with each statement for the way you truly are, not how you might want to be. Think carefully about how you normally think, behave and feel. For example, look at the statement that appears immediately below:

	How I am					
	Agree				Disagree	
	1	2	3	4	5	6
Am completely alert when I wake	O	O	O	O	O	O

The scale is to help you put down what you think is true for you. You have to cross through or tick the circle that describes you. This is what the circles mean:

1 Definitely agree.

2 Agree, but less strongly.

3 On balance, tend to agree.

4 On balance, tend to disagree.

5 Tend to disagree.

6 Definitely disagree.

Do Part 1 of the questionnaire first. Try to ignore the second column, which is about Part 2. How to do Part 2 will be explained later, once you have got to the end of the first column.

For each statement, cross through or tick the circle that is most true for you in the column for 'How I am'.

	Part 1 How I am						Part 2 How I want to be					
	Agree					Disagree	Disagree					Agree
	1	2	3	4	5	6	6	5	4	3	2	1
1. Take chances	Ø	O	O	O	O	O	Ø	O	O	O	O	O
2. Worry about people	O	O	Ø	O	O	O	Ø	O	O	O	O	O
3. Enjoy being alone	O	O	O	O	O	Ø	O	O	Ø	O	O	O
4. Listen more than speak	O	O	O	O	O	Ø	O	O	O	O	O	Ø
5. Rarely feel tired	O	O	O	Ø	O	O	O	O	O	O	O	Ø
6. Have original views	Ø	O	O	O	O	O	O	O	O	O	O	Ø
7. Cautious about change	O	O	Ø	O	O	O	Ø	O	O	O	O	O
8. Unemotional	O	O	O	O	O	Ø	Ø	O	O	O	O	O
9. Seek people to join	O	O	O	O	Ø	O	O	O	O	O	O	Ø
10. Like to be in charge	Ø	O	O	O	O	O	O	O	O	O	O	Ø
11. Sometimes feel weak	Ø	O	O	O	O	O	Ø	O	O	O	O	O
12. Distrust my imagination	O	O	O	O	O	Ø	Ø	O	O	O	O	O
13. Easily distracted	O	O	Ø	O	O	O	Ø	O	O	O	O	O

	Part 1 How I am						Part 2 How I want to be					
	Agree			Disagree			Disagree					Agree
	1	2	3	4	5	6	6	5	4	3	2	1
14. Upset by cruel remarks	X						X					
15. Bored at social events				X			X					
16. Do not argue						X	X					
17. More energy than most	X											X
18. Come up with ideas	X											X
19. Careful	X											X
20. Take tough decisions						X						X
21. Included by others	X											X
22. Often take command	X											X
23. Occasionally need to rest	X											X
24. Hold traditional views						X	X					
25. Bored by routine	X						X					
26. Sensitive to criticism		X					X					
27. Socialize only if I have to			X				X					
28. Accept others' decisions	X											X
29. Highly active	X											X
30. Have invented something	X											X
31. Do not like uncertainty	X						X					
32. Stick to facts	X											X
33. Include others	X											X
34. Influence people	X											X
35. Cannot always cope	X						X					
36. Wary of new ideas						X	X					
37. Like risks			X									X
38. A 'soft-hearted' type	X											X
39. Like my own company	X											X

| | Part 1 How I am | | | | | | Part 2 How I want to be | | | | | |
| | Agree | | | | | Disagree | Disagree | | | | | Agree |
	1	2	3	4	5	6	6	5	4	3	2	1
40. Let others take the lead	○	○	○	○	○	●	●	○	○	○	○	○
41. Always busy	●	○	○	○	○	○	○	○	○	○	●	○
42. Improve the way things work	●	○	○	○	○	○	○	○	○	○	○	●
43. Properly finish things	○	○	○	●	○	○	○	○	○	○	○	●
44. Strong-willed	●	○	○	○	○	○	○	○	○	○	○	●
45. Usually with someone	○	○	○	○	○	●	○	○	○	●	○	○
46. Like my orders followed	●	○	○	○	○	○	○	○	○	○	○	●
47. Lack determination	○	●	○	○	○	○	●	○	○	○	○	○
48. Conventionally minded	○	○	○	○	○	●	●	○	○	○	○	○
49. Changeable	○	○	●	○	○	○	○	○	○	○	○	●
50. Avoid upsetting others	●	○	○	○	○	○	○	○	○	○	○	●
51. Work best alone	●	○	○	○	○	○	●	○	○	○	○	○
52. Tend to hold back	○	○	○	○	○	●	●	○	○	○	○	○
53. Work in my leisure time	○	○	○	○	○	●	●	○	○	○	○	○
54. Get flashes of inspiration	●	○	○	○	○	○	○	○	○	○	○	●
55. Like things to stay the same	○	○	○	○	○	●	●	○	○	○	○	○
56. Deal firmly with people	●	○	○	○	○	○	○	○	○	○	○	●
57. Try to get to know people	○	○	○	●	○	○	○	○	○	○	○	●
58. Take control of people	○	○	○	○	○	●	○	○	○	○	○	●
59. Sometimes want to give up	●	○	○	○	○	○	●	○	○	○	○	○
60. Fearful of change	○	○	●	○	○	○	●	○	○	○	○	○
	Now read below about how to do Part 2.						Now go on to how to mark your scores.					

Part 2: How I want to be

This part is about how you would want to see yourself – the way you would be if you did not have restrictions that held you back. It is not necessarily about being a wildly different type of person, but simply about the person you would like to be. It is about possibility and potential as opposed to how you perceive yourself at present.

You have to say whether you agree or disagree with each statement for the way you truly want to be. It is all right for you to use imagination and to shrug off any feelings you may have about lack of confidence or 'showing off' or being modest. Answer the questions in relation to how you would like to view your 'ideal self'.

The statements are the same as for Part 1, but the scale is now the other way around, with 6 on the left side and 1 on the right. Apart from the numbers the statements are the same as in Part 1.

	How I want to be					
	Disagree					Agree
	6	5	4	3	2	1
Am completely alert when I wake	O	O	O	O	O	O

To remind you, this is what the circles mean:

1 Definitely agree.

2 Agree, but less strongly.

3 On balance, tend to agree.

4 On balance, tend to disagree.

5 Tend to disagree.

6 Definitely disagree.

For each statement, cross through or tick the circle that is true for how you want to be.

Go back to the top of the test and begin the right-hand column. Ignore the answers you have already made on the left. If you like, cover them up as you work down the right-hand column.

Marking Parts 1 and 2 of the six-factor personality test

The marking schemes below show you how to obtain your results from both parts of the questionnaire. Start with the first table below, for 'Casual'. This shows you each question and whether the ticks or circles you marked obtained a score.

For example, look back at the way you completed Part 1 of the questionnaire, 'How I am'. The table below tells you that, if you marked circle 1 or 2 on question 1, you get a score of 1. Otherwise, you do not score.

Then do the same with question 7. If you have crossed through circle 4, 5 or 6 you score 1, so put a 1 in the score tally column. Otherwise, leave the space blank.

Do the same with the other questions in the group, and complete all the tables. Finally, you can count up the number of times you have scored. Your result will range somewhere between 0 and 10.

For Part 2 of the questionnaire, 'How I want to be', marking is done in exactly the same way.

Casual			
Question number	These crossed circles score	Part 1 How I am	Part 2 How I want to be
1	1 or 2		
7	4, 5 or 6		
13	1, 2 or 3		
19	3, 4, 5 or 6		
25	1, 2 or 3		
31	4, 5 or 6		
37	1 or 2		
43	5 or 6		
49	1, 2, 3 or 4		
55	5 or 6		
	Total scores =		

Tough			
Question number	These crossed circles score	Part 1 How I am	Part 2 How I want to be
2	4, 5 or 6	_____	_____
8	1 or 2	_____	_____
14	4, 5 or 6	_____	_____
20	1, 2 or 3	_____	_____
26	5 or 6	_____	_____
32	1 or 2	_____	_____
38	5 or 6	_____	_____
44	1 or 2	_____	_____
50	4, 5 or 6	_____	_____
56	1 or 2	_____	_____
	Total scores =	_____	_____

Independent			
Question number	These crossed circles score	Part 1 How I am	Part 2 How I want to be
3	1, 2 or 3	_____	_____
9	3, 4, 5 or 6	_____	_____
15	1, 2, 3 or 4	_____	_____
21	3, 4, 5 or 6	_____	_____
27	1, 2, 3 or 4	_____	_____
33	3, 4, 5 or 6	_____	_____
39	1 or 2	_____	_____
45	5 or 6	_____	_____
51	1, 2, 3 or 4	_____	_____
57	3, 4, 5 or 6	_____	_____
	Total scores =	_____	_____

Controlling			
Question number	These crossed circles score	Part 1 How I am	Part 2 How I want to be
4	4, 5 or 6	_____	_____
10	1 or 2	_____	_____
16	5 or 6	_____	_____
22	1 or 2	_____	_____
28	5 or 6	_____	_____
34	1 or 2	_____	_____
40	5 or 6	_____	_____
46	1 or 2	_____	_____
52	5 or 6	_____	_____
58	1 or 2	_____	_____
	Total scores =	_____	_____

Energetic			
Question number	These crossed circles score	Part 1 How I am	Part 2 How I want to be
5	1, 2 or 3	_____	_____
11	5 or 6	_____	_____
17	1, 2 or 3	_____	_____
23	5 or 6	_____	_____
29	1 or 2	_____	_____
35	5 or 6	_____	_____
41	1 or 2	_____	_____
47	5 or 6	_____	_____
53	1 or 2	_____	_____
59	5 or 6	_____	_____
	Total scores =	_____	_____

Creative			
Question number	These crossed circles score	Part 1 How I am	Part 2 How I want to be
6	1, 2 or 3	_____	_____
12	4, 5 or 6	_____	_____
18	1 or 2	_____	_____
24	4, 5 or 6	_____	_____
30	1, 2 or 3	_____	_____
36	5 or 6	_____	_____
42	1 or 2	_____	_____
48	4, 5 or 6	_____	_____
54	1 or 2	_____	_____
60	4, 5 or 6	_____	_____
	Total scores =	_____	_____

The scores you have obtained above should now be placed in the six personality factors chart below. For the scores in Part 1 make a circle around the corresponding number in the chart. For example, if you obtained a score of '3' in the 'Casual' table, Part 1, 'How I am', place a circle around the figure '3' in the chart. Place circles round the other figures in the chart to show all your scores in Part 1.

Then do the same for your results in Part 2, 'How I want to be', only this time mark the results with a cross.

Draw a line joining up the circles in the graph. Then draw a separate line joining the crosses. This makes it easy to see how much divergence there is between any two scores on the same dimensions.

Six personality factors chart

1   Casual

Cautious   Impulsive

0   1   2   3   4   5   –   6   7   8   9   10

2   Tough

Soft   Tough

0   1   2   3   4   5   –   6   7   8   9   10

3   Independent

Sociable   Detached

0   1   2   3   4   5   –   6   7   8   9   10

4   Controlling

Unassuming   Authoritative

0   1   2   3   4   5   –   6   7   8   9   10

5   Energetic

Passive   Active

0   1   2   3   4   5   –   6   7   8   9   10

6   Creative

Conservative   Innovative

0   1   2   3   4   5   –   6   7   8   9   10

What the six factors measure

The test investigates the critical ways in which you deal with situations that confront you. Everyone has tasks that they have to perform, every moment of every day. Some of these you do consciously, though most are performed subconsciously. They are simply part of the behavioural repertoire you have built up over time. They are your preferred ways of dealing with the world and its people.

There are no moral judgements about what it is 'best' to be. Ultimately, what is 'best' for you may well be different from what is 'best' for others, but it is what you want.

The six factors are all separate, but all impact upon each other to blend to produce your own unique style. They produce within you an amazingly diverse and dynamic individual. Explanation of how they can work for you and the directions they suggest for you will be given later on in this chapter.

Remember that, of the words and phrases below that are associated with each factor, not all will apply exactly to you. Some will have more relevance than others. It is up to you to establish in what way your score has meaning for you, interpreting it for yourself and deriving your own conclusions as to what has meaning for you and the way you lead your life, and whether there is a direction to which you want to change.

Therefore the descriptions that follow should be treated as references or as guides to your thinking and analysis. You might like to underline those descriptions that you think describe you in some way in certain circumstances. 'Average' scores avoid the extremes of the description or have some of the characteristics of both poles of the factor.

It may help to tick or in some way highlight the paragraphs below that relate to your own scores.

Your organization

Both factors in this dimension assess your style in dealing with issues and all types of problem solving, whether personal or interpersonal, emotional or factual.

Factor 1: casual – cautious or impulsive

Lower scores on factor 1 reveal a 'cautious' approach, possibly: alert, careful, chary, circumspect, deliberate, discreet, guarded, heedful, painstaking, prudent, reluctant, safe, scrupulous, softly-softly, suspicious, tentative, unadventurous, vigilant and wary.

At the other end of the scale, higher scores suggest: apathetic, blasé, chancy, dangerous, hazardous, impulsive, informal, irregular, random, risky, speculative, tricky, uncertain and venturesome.

Factor 2: tough – soft or tough

Lower scores on factor 2 suggest passivity: accommodating, compliant, docile, emotional, enduring, feeling-minded, lenient, non-violent, patient, receptive, sensitive, soft, unassertive and understanding.

Higher scores suggest toughness: active, factual, firm, lively, impatient, intolerant, obstinate, pugnacious, ruthless, strong, unbending and vigorous.

Your interaction

The two factors in this dimension assess how much you mix with people and, to the degree you are with others, how influential you are. These factors are about your preferred ways of being with people and relating to them.

Factor 3: independent – sociable or detached

Lower scores on factor 3 suggest participation: accessible, affable, companionable, extrovert, familiar, fraternal, friendly, getting-together, gregarious, mixing, outgoing, party-loving.

Higher scores suggest social detachment: autonomous, free, independent, self-contained, unbiased, unfriendly, unsociable and withdrawn.

Factor 4: controlling – unassuming or authoritative

Low scores on factor 4 suggest you take a low profile: diffident, humble, meek, modest, natural, quiet, restrained, retiring and unpresuming.

Higher scores suggest authority: commanding, confident, decisive, determined, dominating, manipulative, outspoken, ruling, straightforward, supervising and taking charge.

Your enthusiasm

Firstly, in this dimension, your result looks at how much effort you put into achieving, as this is an essential part of your approach to life. High energy simply exists as a force, but also has to be applied usefully or it is wasted or even misdirected. At the same time, low energy may well be sufficient to achieve what is wanted in a manner that has a result in contentment.

Secondly comes your creativity. This result is about how far you are likely to be original in coming up with new ideas and being inspired. The opposite side of this is to rely upon what is familiar and comfortable. Both approaches can succeed, but of course in different ways; being on the conservative side will almost guarantee some achievement, even though it may not be world-shattering, whereas out-and-out innovation may turn out to be irrelevant!

Factor 5: energetic – passive or active

Low scores are associated with passivity: calm, docile, inactive, indifferent, lethargic, mild, non-aggressive, peaceful, quiet, resigned, serene, slow, undisturbed and unperturbed.

High scores describe a more energetic, driving approach: acting, animated, bustling, doing, engaged, enterprising, industrious, on the go, roused, strenuous, vigorous and zestful.

Factor 6: creative – conservative or innovative

Low scores relate to conservatism in your style: conventional, hide-bound, middle-of-the-road, moderate, non-progressive, sober, traditional and unexaggerated.

High scores are associated with a more innovative approach: fresh, ground-breaking, imaginative, inventive, modernizing, new, original, progressive and revolutionary.

These three dimensions, and six factors, relate to your typical approach to work matters that burden you and to all areas where you have to get something done or resolve matters. They have to do with the manner you adopt when you attempt to do something. The style with which you try to achieve is apparent in almost everything you do, whether at work or at home, the way you deal with things and the way you relate to issues with people.

Interpretation of your results

1. Casual

Scores 0, 1, 2, 3
You are likely to be practical and down-to-earth. You do not like to take chances. Slow to change, you are consistent and prudent, but wary of the unknown. You sometimes are unobservant, lack confidence and are overcautious.

Scores 4, 5, 6, 7
You take measured risks. You are open to possibilities, but also dependable. Though unlikely to 'lose your head', you are keen to have some change and variety as well. Generally, you balance expressiveness with mature control of emotions.

Scores 8, 9, 10
You enthusiastically respond to new possibilities. You like change and are always looking over the horizon, so there is a danger you do not complete things. You can be impetuous and take chances. Lacking inhibition, you can be opinionated and possibly distracted by the latest events.

2. Tough

Scores 0, 1, 2, 3
You are insightful and sensitive to people, situations and the world around you. You think carefully about emotional situations. You can become upset and frustrated, dwelling upon setbacks. You can be self-critical and suspicious of others' motives.

Scores 4, 5, 6, 7
You take account of tasks as well as feelings. A good planner and reliable, you are also attentive to others. You express your thoughts upon issues without blaming others. You take reasonable initiatives on your own, whilst recognizing the talents that others have.

Scores 8, 9, 10
Solid and predictable, you are steady and well organized, using time efficiently. You can appear emotionally inexpressive – tough or cool. Rarely defeated by difficulties, owing to your common sense, you are adaptable, self-reliant and industrious.

3. Independent

Scores 0, 1, 2, 3
You are participative and cooperative. You persevere with people and possibly have a need to be included. You are kind and dependable, likely to combine your own initiative with that of others.

Scores 4, 5, 6, 7
Whilst you enjoy others' company, you are capable of working alone. You preserve your own interests whilst sharing. You mix easily with many people and can create a balance by adapting to them quickly.

Scores 8, 9, 10
You are inclined to be reserved and serious. At the extreme you can be ill at ease socially. Indifferent to others, you can sometimes seem shy, sometimes impatient or aloof. You prefer your own company. Generally, you are self-contained and undemonstrative.

4. Controlling

Scores 0, 1, 2, 3
You are mild-mannered. Sometimes you are reticent and deferential. You are cautious about asserting yourself. You tend to wait to see what is happening or what is expected of you. You may lack confidence or simply prefer to do things your own way.

Scores 4, 5, 6, 7
You are determined without an obvious show of force. You are positive and encouraging without being demanding. Your style is cooperative rather than dominant. You take responsibility when the situation warrants it, but prefer to share decisions.

Scores 8, 9, 10
You are competitive and take the lead. Self-assured, even 'pushy', you like responsibility. You do best when you have an audience or a following. Assertive and impatient, you are often persuasive.

5. Energetic

Scores 0, 1, 2, 3
You may find it difficult to persist with a task for long. You can be distracted or take up another thing that appears to be easier. You tend to doubt yourself. You lack resolve. It may be that you think of possible consequences, which makes you refrain. Sometimes you cannot make the effort or perhaps prefer to cut corners and take an easier route.

Scores 4, 5, 6, 7
You have the energy to do most things. You balance action with thought. Willing and committed in the short term, you can nevertheless feel pressure over time. You are ambitious, but not at any cost. You care what others think.

Scores 8, 9, 10
You are impatient to achieve. You have a restless though positive driving energy and commitment. You spot ways of succeeding. You get on with things and want to make them happen. You can be unforgiving, stubborn, pushy and aggressive.

6. Creative

Scores 0, 1, 2, 3
Factually minded, you value tried-and-tested experience. You are traditional, having a realistic view of what is correct. You perceive situations in a straightforward way and are pleased by the way things are. You like continuity, improving upon what you have, as opposed to being radical.

Scores 4, 5, 6, 7
You like to see change, but not for its own sake; you like to see the purpose in novelty. You will use new ideas, not originate them. You possess insight, but adapt rather than pursue ideas in depth. You enjoy new things and ideas, but like these to be useful.

Scores 8, 9, 10
You are expressive and have many interests. You challenge the way things are. You can be idealistic and may have high standards. Your approach may be unusual. Complex, you can have strong opinions. You are critical and sceptical. You value ideas and may have some of your own.

Analysis of scores

You will find much to think about when you look at the discrepancies between your scores for how you are and those for how you want to be. Even where there are no large discrepancies, or even minor ones, it is worth asking yourself why you should want to make a change in one direction or the other.

The exercise will be of most value to you if you carefully think through your scores and what they signify in your life. The exercise becomes more meaningful if you write down your thoughts in the appropriate space. This assists in making your thoughts and feelings more concrete and thereby easier to understand.

The fear of being the 'real you'

This book is founded on the premise that the person you want to be is more likely to be the real you than the person you are now! This is because what we perceive in our imagination is, in fact, a disclosure of our potential.

Of course, there is no obligation to act on what you know is possible for you; there may be many reasons why you might choose not to do something you want to do. But making an informed choice is preferable to making an excuse, pretending you cannot do what you want or blaming others. If there is nothing holding you back apart from confidence, then it is worth bringing any fears you have about change to the front of your mind. Confronting fears objectively often reveals how irrational they are; once they are identified, you are likely to see a way of overcoming them.

Whilst it is true that your own experience of fear about changing yourself to be more like the person you really are will be unique, owing to your own history, it is also true that all human beings have the same fundamental fears. They are very simple, but also very powerful; they are the source of all our emotions. They are:

- fear of being ignored;
- fear of seeming stupid;
- fear of not being liked;
- fear of letting people down;
- fear of not being able to cope.

Think through your emotions and the fears you have as you work through the following analysis. Writing what you feel about your results is a good way to make clear those issues that are relevant to your development. Making these concrete in written form allows you to focus upon them in a meaningful way and, in particular, helps to prevent you from pushing them once again to the back of your mind. It is in the back of your mind that they are most bothersome, as they usually continue to affect you and your behaviour, for example making you resentful or irritable, without being conscious why.

You may consider that the word 'fear' is too strong a word. Milder words may be: apprehension, concern, disquiet, doubt, dread, foreboding, qualm, unease, unsureness, worry. They are all states of anxious premonition that may describe what stops you from changing in the way you want. 'Fear' is just the collective word we use to describe all shades of this state of lack of confidence that holds you back.

1. Casual

a.	How I am	How I want to be
Scores	0, 1, 2, 3	0, 1, 2, 3

How you are appears to be how you want to be. You like to be cautious, even though you may miss some chances. However, if there is a difference of even one point between the two scores, ask yourself whether this signifies anything. For example, though you do not seem to want to change very much, why might you want to change in the indicated direction, moving one way rather than the other?

In respect of this aspect:

Have you ever tried to be more or less venturesome? If not, why?

....

Have you any fear about changing?

....

What is the worst that could happen and how would you deal with that?

....

b.	How I am	How I want to be
Scores	0, 1, 2, 3	4, 5, 6, 7, 8, 9, 10

You are practical and down-to-earth, but would like to be more open-minded and adventurous in your approach to tasks.

In respect of this aspect:

Why do you not like yourself the way you are?

....

What fear do you have about changing?

....

What is the worst that could happen and how would you deal with that?

....

c.	How I am	How I want to be
Scores	4, 5, 6, 7	0, 1, 2, 3

You take measured risks and are unlikely to 'lose your head', but you would like to have more control and prudence.
    In respect of this aspect:

Why do you not like yourself the way you are?

....

What fear do you have about changing?

....

What is the worst that could happen and how would you deal with that?

....

d.	How I am	How I want to be
Scores	4, 5, 6, 7	4, 5, 6, 7

You take measured risks, being open to possibilities, but also dependable. If there is a difference of even one point between the two scores, ask yourself whether this signifies anything. For example, though you do not seem to want to change very much, if at all, why might you want to move one way or the other?

In respect of this aspect:

Have you ever tried to be more or less venturesome? If not, why?

....

What fear do you have about changing?

....

Has there been a time you were venturesome and failed? How did you deal with that?

....

e.	How I am	How I want to be
Scores	4, 5, 6, 7	8, 9, 10

You are open to possibilities, but would like to respond more enthusiastically to new possibilities and take more risk.
   In respect of this aspect:

Why do you not like yourself the way you are?

....

What fear do you have about changing?

....

What is the worst that could happen and how would you deal with that?

....

f.	How I am	How I want to be
Scores	8, 9, 10	8, 9, 10

You like change and take chances. If there is a difference of even one point between the two scores, ask yourself whether this signifies anything. For example, though you do not seem to want to change very much, why might you want to change in the indicated direction, moving one way rather than the other?

In respect of this aspect:

Have you ever tried to be less venturesome? If not, why?

. . . .

Have you any fear about changing to a different style?

. . . .

Has there been a time you were less venturesome and failed? How did you deal with that?

. . . .

g.	How I am	How I want to be
Scores	8, 9, 10	0, 1, 2, 3, 4, 5, 6, 7

You are impetuous and take chances, but seem to want to be less so. You like taking risks, but think you should have a more measured approach.

In respect of this aspect:

Why do you not like yourself the way you are?

. . . .

What fear do you have about changing?

. . . .

What is the worst that could happen and how would you deal with that?

. . . .

2. Tough

a.	How I am	How I want to be
Scores	0, 1, 2, 3	0, 1, 2, 3

You approach problems with careful awareness of people and their feelings. You may dwell upon setbacks and be self-critical and suspicious of others. If there is a difference of even one point between the two scores, ask yourself whether this signifies anything. For example, though you do not seem to want to change very much, why might you want to change even a little?

In respect of this aspect:

Have you ever tried to be more or less tough or unfeeling? If not, why?

....

What fear do you have about changing?

....

Has there been a time you were tough-minded and failed? How did you deal with that?

....

b.	How I am	How I want to be
Scores	0, 1, 2, 3	4, 5, 6, 7, 8, 9, 10

Imaginative and insightful, you approach problems with careful awareness. You may dwell upon setbacks and be self-critical and suspicious of others. You want to take more account of tasks as much as feelings.

In respect of this aspect:

Why do you not like yourself the way you are?

....

What fear do you have about changing?

....

What is the worst that could happen and how would you deal with that?

....

c.	How I am	How I want to be
Scores	4, 5, 6, 7	0, 1, 2, 3

You take account of tasks as well as feelings. You express your thoughts upon issues without blaming others. You take reasonable initiatives on your own, whilst recognizing the talents that others have. However, you would like to be more insightful so you approach problems with greater awareness of people and their feelings.

In respect of this aspect:

Why do you not like yourself the way you are?

. . . .

What fear do you have about changing?

. . . .

What is the worst that could happen and how would you deal with that?

. . . .

d.	How I am	How I want to be
Scores	4, 5, 6, 7	4, 5, 6, 7

You take account of tasks as well as feelings. Measured and reliable, you are also attentive to others. You express your thoughts upon issues without blaming others. You take reasonable initiatives on your own, whilst recognizing the talents that others have. If there is a difference of even one point between the two scores, ask yourself whether this signifies anything. For example, though you do not seem to want to change very much, why might you want to change in the indicated direction, moving one way rather than the other?

In respect of this aspect:

Have you ever tried to be more sensitive or more unfeeling? If not, why?

. . . .

What fear do you have about changing?

. . . .

Has there been a time you were venturesome and failed? How did you deal with that?

. . . .

e.	How I am	How I want to be
Scores	4, 5, 6, 7	8, 9, 10

You take account of tasks as well as feelings. You express your thoughts upon issues without blaming others. You take reasonable initiatives on your own, whilst recognizing the talents that others have. However, you would like to take people's feelings less into account and have a tougher approach.

In respect of this aspect:

Why do you not like yourself the way you are?

. . . .

What fear do you have about changing?

. . . .

What is the worst that could happen and how would you deal with that?

. . . .

f.	How I am	How I want to be
Scores	8, 9, 10	8, 9, 10

You are steady and well organized, using time efficiently. You can appear emotionally unexpressive – tough or cool. Rarely defeated by difficulties, owing to your common sense, you are adaptable, self-reliant and industrious. If there is a difference of even one point between the two scores, ask yourself whether this signifies anything. For example, though you do not seem to want to change very much, why might you want to change in the indicated direction, moving one way rather than the other?

In respect of this aspect:

Have you ever tried to be less tough or unfeeling? If not, why?

. . . .

What fear do you have about changing?

. . . .

Has there been a time you acted differently and failed? How did you deal with that?

. . . .

g.	How I am	How I want to be
Scores	8, 9, 10	0, 1, 2, 3, 4, 5, 6, 7

Using time efficiently, you can appear emotionally inexpressive – tough or cool. Rarely defeated by difficulties, owing to your common sense, you are self-reliant and industrious. However, you would like to take account of feelings rather more. You see benefits in being attentive to others and expressing your feelings more without blame.

In respect of this aspect:

Why do you not like yourself the way you are?

. . . .

What fear do you have about changing?

. . . .

What is the worst that could happen and how would you deal with that?

. . . .

3. *Independent*

a.   How I am   How I want to be

Scores   0, 1, 2, 3   0, 1, 2, 3

You are participative and cooperative. You persevere with people because you like to be included a great deal. You do not want to change much, if at all, but even the indication of a slight change might be significant: why might you want to be even a little less or more social?

In respect of this aspect:

Have you ever tried to be less interactive? If not, why?

· ·

What fear do you have about changing?

· ·

Has there been a time you tried to be more independent and failed? Why was that?

· ·

b.   How I am   How I want to be

Scores   0, 1, 2, 3   4, 5, 6, 7, 8, 9, 10

You are participative and cooperative. You persevere with people and like to be included. Whilst you enjoy others' company, you want to have more time to yourself. In some ways you want to be more self-reliant.

In respect of this aspect:

Why would you like yourself more if you were more independent?

· ·

What fear do you have about changing?

· ·

What is the worst that could happen and how would you deal with that?

. . . .

c.	How I am	How I want to be
Scores	4, 5, 6, 7	0, 1, 2, 3

Whilst you enjoy others' company, you are capable of working alone. You preserve your own interests whilst sharing. You want to be more participative and have people include you more.

In respect of this aspect:

Why do you want to be more social?

. . . .

What fear do you have about changing?

. . . .

What is the worst that could happen and how would you deal with that?

. . . .

d.	How I am	How I want to be
Scores	4, 5, 6, 7	4, 5, 6, 7

Whilst you enjoy others' company, you are capable of working alone. You preserve your own interests whilst sharing. However, if there is even a small difference between the two scores, ask yourself whether this signifies anything. What might you get out of even a slight change in your behaviour?

In respect of this aspect:

Have you ever tried to be more or less social? What feeling did you get?

. . . .

What fear do you have about changing?

. . . .

Has there been a time you were more or less social and failed? How did you deal with that?

. . . .

e.	How I am	How I want to be
Scores	4, 5, 6, 7	8, 9, 10

Whilst you enjoy others' company, you are capable of working alone. You preserve your own interests whilst sharing. You would like to be more reserved and self-contained.

In respect of this aspect:

What do you not like about yourself the way you are?

. . . .

What fear do you have about changing?

. . . .

What is the worst that could happen and how would you deal with that?

. . . .

f.	How I am	How I want to be
Scores	8, 9, 10	8, 9, 10

You are inclined to be reserved and serious. You can sometimes seem shy, impatient or aloof. Generally, you are self-contained and undemonstrative and do not appear to want to change much, if at all. However, if there is even a small difference between the two scores, ask yourself whether this signifies anything. What might you get out of even a slight change in your behaviour?

In respect of this aspect:

Have you ever tried to interact with people more? If not, why?

What fear do you have about changing?

How do others feel about your independence?

g.	How I am	How I want to be
Scores	8, 9, 10	0, 1, 2, 3, 4, 5, 6, 7

You are inclined to be reserved and serious. You can sometimes seem shy, impatient or aloof. Generally, you are self-contained and undemonstrative, but you would like to change this aspect, becoming more easy-going and participative.

In respect of this aspect:

Why do you not like yourself the way you are?

What fear do you have about changing?

What is the worst that could happen and how would you deal with that?

4. Controlling

a.	How I am	How I want to be
Scores	0, 1, 2, 3	0, 1, 2, 3

You are mild-mannered. Sometimes you are reticent and deferential. You are cautious about asserting yourself. You tend to wait to see what is happening or what is expected of you or simply prefer to do things your own way. However, if there is even a small difference between the two scores, ask yourself whether this signifies anything. What might you get out of even a slight change in your behaviour?

In respect of this aspect:

Have you ever tried to be more controlling? If not, why?

. . . .

What fear do you have about changing?

. . . .

Has there been a time you took control and failed? How did you deal with that?

. . . .

b.	How I am	How I want to be
Scores	0, 1, 2, 3	4, 5, 6, 7, 8, 9, 10

You are mild-mannered. Maybe you are reticent and deferential, but certainly cautious about asserting yourself. You tend to 'wait and see' rather than take charge. But you would like to be bolder in this regard, taking the lead and asserting yourself more.

In respect of this aspect:

What do you not like about yourself the way you are?

. . . .

What fear do you have about changing?

. . . .

What is the worst that could happen and how would you deal with that?

. . . .

c.	How I am	How I want to be
Scores	4, 5, 6, 7	0, 1, 2, 3

You are encouraging without being demanding. Your style is cooperative rather than dominant. You like to share decisions. However, you seem to think you are too assertive. You would like to be more cautious or perhaps allow others to take more control.

In respect of this aspect:

What do you not like about yourself the way you are now?

. . . .

What fear do you have about changing?

. . . .

What is the worst that could happen and how would you deal with that?

. . . .

d.	How I am	How I want to be
Scores	4, 5, 6, 7	4, 5, 6, 7

You are encouraging without being demanding. Your style is cooperative rather than dominant. You like to share decisions. However, if there is even a small difference between the two scores, ask yourself whether this signifies anything. What might you get out of even a slight change in your behaviour?

In respect of this aspect:

Have you ever tried to be more or less controlling? If not, why?

. . . .

What do you think others might think if you acted differently in this regard?

. . . .

Has there been a time you were more or less controlling and failed? How did you deal with that?

. . . .

e.	How I am	How I want to be
Scores	4, 5, 6, 7	8, 9, 10

You are encouraging without being demanding. Your style is cooperative rather than dominant. You like to share decisions. However, you want to take the lead a good deal more.

In respect of this aspect:

In what way do you not like yourself the way you are?

. . . .

What fear do you have about changing?

. . . .

How do you think other people would feel if you changed in the way you want?

. . . .

f.	How I am	How I want to be
Scores	8, 9, 10	8, 9, 10

You are competitive and take the lead. Assertive and impatient, you are often persuasive and enjoy being in a position of control. However, even if there is no difference between the scores, but definitely if there is even a slight one, ask yourself whether this signifies anything.

In respect of this aspect:

Have you ever tried to be less controlling? If not, why?

. . . .

What fear do you have about changing?

. . . .

Has there been a time you were less controlling and failed? How did you deal with that?

. . . .

g.	How I am	How I want to be
Scores	8, 9, 10	0, 1, 2, 3, 4, 5, 6, 7

You are competitive and take the lead. Assertive and impatient, you are often persuasive, but you would like to be less aggressive and more participative. Without being so forceful you would like to obtain the response you want from others.

In respect of this aspect:

What do you not like about yourself the way you are?

. . . .

What fear do you have about changing?

. . . .

What is the worst that could happen and how would you deal with that?

. . . .

5. Energetic

a.	How I am	How I want to be
Scores	0, 1, 2, 3	0, 1, 2, 3

You may find it difficult to persist with a task for long. You lack resolve. Sometimes you cannot make the effort or prefer to cut corners and take an easier route. If there is a difference of even one point between the two scores, ask yourself whether this signifies anything. For example, though you do not seem to want to change very much, why might you want to change in the indicated direction, moving one way rather than the other?

In respect of this aspect:

Have you ever tried to be more or less energetic? If not, why?

. . . .

Have you any fear about changing?

. . . .

Has there been a time you were more active? Did this fail you in some way?

. . . .

b.	How I am	How I want to be
Scores	0, 1, 2, 3	4, 5, 6, 7, 8, 9, 10

You may find it difficult to persist with a task for long. You lack resolve. Sometimes you cannot make the effort or prefer to cut corners and take an easier route. You would like the energy to do more in order to achieve more of what you often know you are capable of doing.

In respect of this aspect:

Why do you not like yourself the way you are?

. . . .

What fear do you have about changing?

. . . .

What is the worst that could happen and how would you deal with that?

. . . .

c.	How I am	How I want to be
Scores	4, 5, 6, 7	0, 1, 2, 3

You have the energy to do most things. You balance action with thought. You are ambitious, but not at any cost. But you would like to take things easier, be less enthusiastic or not persist with things so long or not wear yourself out so much.

In respect of this aspect:

What do you consider you would get from having less energy?

. . . .

What fear do you have about changing?

. . . .

What is the worst that could happen and how would you deal with that?

. . . .

d.	How I am	How I want to be
Scores	4, 5, 6, 7	4, 5, 6, 7

You have the energy to do most things. You balance action with thought. You are ambitious, but not at any cost. If there is a difference of even one point between the two scores, ask yourself whether this signifies anything. For example, though you do not seem to want to change very much, why might you want to change in the indicated direction, moving one way rather than the other?

In respect of this aspect:

Have you ever tried to be more or less energetic? If not, what stops you trying?

. . . .

What fear do you have about changing?

. . . .

Has there been a time you were more or less energetic and failed? How was that experience?

. . . .

e.	How I am	How I want to be
Scores	4, 5, 6, 7	8, 9, 10

You have the energy to do most things. You balance action with thought. You are ambitious, but not at any cost. You want to make more things happen. You think you would do better to be less patient and more assertive.

In respect of this aspect:

Why do you not like yourself the way you are?

. . . .

What fear do you have about changing?

. . . .

What is the worst that could happen and how would you deal with that?

. . . .

f.	How I am	How I want to be
Scores	8, 9, 10	8, 9, 10

You are impatient to achieve and want to make things happen. You can be unforgiving, stubborn, pushy and aggressive. If there is a difference of even one point between the two scores, ask yourself whether this signifies anything. For example, though you do not seem to want to change very much, why might you want to change in the indicated direction, moving one way rather than the other?

In respect of this aspect:

Have you ever tried to be less driving of yourself and, perhaps, others?

. . . .

What fear do you have about changing? Is it that you fear you might fail to cope, if you did?

. . . .

Has there been a time you let go and failed? How did you deal with that?

. . . .

g.	How I am	How I want to be
Scores	8, 9, 10	0, 1, 2, 3, 4, 5, 6, 7

You are impatient to achieve and want to make things happen. You can be unforgiving, stubborn, pushy and aggressive. You would like to slow down a little, show more tolerance and take a more balanced approach, putting more consideration into actions you take.

In respect of this aspect:

Why do you not like yourself the way you are?

....

What fear do you have about changing?

....

What is the worst that could happen and how would you deal with that?

....

6. Creative

a.	How I am	How I want to be
Scores	0, 1, 2, 3	0, 1, 2, 3

You value tried-and-tested experience. You are traditional, having a realistic view of what is correct. You perceive situations in a straightforward way. If there is a difference of even one point between the two scores, ask yourself whether this signifies anything. For example, though you do not seem to want to change very much, why might you want to change in the indicated direction, moving one way rather than the other?

In respect of this aspect:

Have you ever tried to be more innovative? If not, why?

....

What fear do you have about changing?

....

Has there been a time you were innovative and failed? How did you deal with that?

. . . .

b.	How I am	How I want to be
Scores	0, 1, 2, 3	4, 5, 6, 7, 8, 9, 10

You value tried-and-tested experience. You are traditional, having a realistic view of what is correct. You perceive situations in a straightforward way. You want to be more readily accepting of new ideas, perhaps even see if you might have some ideas of your own.

In respect of this aspect:

Why do you not like yourself the way you are?

. . . .

What fear do you have about changing?

. . . .

What is the worst that could happen and how would you deal with that?

. . . .

c.	How I am	How I want to be
Scores	4, 5, 6, 7	0, 1, 2, 3

You like to see change, but not for its own sake. You will use new ideas, not originate them. You possess insight, but adapt rather than pursue ideas in depth. You value tried-and-tested experience. You are traditional, having a realistic view of what is correct. You perceive situations in a straightforward way.

In respect of this aspect:

Why do you not like yourself the way you are?

. . . .

What fear do you have about changing?

· ·

What is the worst that could happen and how would you deal with that?

· ·

d.	How I am	How I want to be
Scores	4, 5, 6, 7	4, 5, 6, 7

You like to see change, but not for its own sake. You will use new ideas, not originate them. You possess insight, but adapt rather than pursue ideas in depth. If there is a difference of even one point between the two scores, ask yourself whether this signifies anything. For example, though you do not seem to want to change very much, why might you want to change in the indicated direction, moving one way rather than the other?

In respect of this aspect:

Have you ever tried to be more or less creative? If not, why?

· ·

What fear do you have about changing?

· ·

Has there been a time you were too creative or not creative enough? Do you feel safer keeping to the middle of the road?

· ·

e.	How I am	How I want to be
Scores	4, 5, 6, 7	8, 9, 10

You like to see change, but not for its own sake. You will use new ideas, not originate them. You possess insight, but adapt rather than pursue ideas in depth. You feel you could be more expressive, develop the creative, critical side of yourself and have the chance to express your ideas.

In respect of this aspect:

Why do you not like yourself the way you are?

. . . .

What fear do you have about changing?

. . . .

What is the worst that could happen and how would you deal with that?

. . . .

f.	How I am	How I want to be
Scores	8, 9, 10	8, 9, 10

You are expressive, with many interests. Complex, you can have strong opinions. You are critical and sceptical. You value ideas and may have some of your own. If there is a difference of even one point between the two scores, ask yourself whether this signifies anything. For example, though you do not seem to want to change very much, why might you want to change in the indicated direction, moving one way rather than the other?

In respect of this aspect:

What would you lose if you were more conservative?

. . . .

What fear do you have about changing?

. . . .

Has there been a time you were more conservative? What did you not like about being that way?

. . . .

g.	How I am	How I want to be
Scores	8, 9, 10	0, 1, 2, 3, 4, 5, 6, 7

You are expressive, with many interests. Complex, you can have strong opinions. You are critical and sceptical. You value ideas and may have some of your own. You want to be more straightforward and realistic, perhaps less carried away and more down-to-earth.

In respect of this aspect:

Why do you not like yourself the way you are?

. . . .

What fear do you have about changing?

. . . .

What is the worst that could happen and how would you deal with that?

. . . .

Action plan

Looking over your analysis:

Am I being honest with myself?

. . . .

What excuses do I make?

. . . .

Am I making myself a victim?

. . . .

Are there ways I blame others for the way I am?

. . . .

What are the common threads that emerge?

. . . .

What do I want to do about these?

....

Am I going to get feedback from people who know me? Who and when?

....

Gaining feedback

The value of getting feedback from another person or lots of people is to challenge your view. People may see you differently from the way you see yourself. This is not to determine who is right or wrong, but why different perceptions arise. You may be fooling yourself, or maybe the other person does not perceive you clearly.

However, differences in perceptions can very easily lead to misunderstandings. For example, if you do not see yourself as aggressive, whilst the other person does, the other person may say nothing and become passive, leading you to think that he or she likes you that way, whereas the truth is that the other person has simply ceased to bother. Then you blame him or her for 'letting you do everything', whereas the other person thinks it is what you want!

Feedback questionnaire

Get someone who is important to you to complete the questionnaire for how that person sees you. It is probably better for the person to complete it for how he or she thinks you are rather than how you want to be, as that is more difficult, though the person can do it that way too if you or he or she wishes. Once you have the person's perceptions for how he or she thinks you are you can compare the scores with your own. Where you want to change your behaviour it is useful to discuss what your fears may be about changing. Such discussions often lead to insights about the possibilities of change, resolving barriers and making change potentially more possible than you ever thought.

My perception of...
How he/she is

In this questionnaire, be honest about how you now see the person. It is about how he or she is at this time in his or her life. It is not about how you imagine the person could be or would like to be. Take a good, hard look at the person; it is especially important to be honest, even if there are things you do not like so much and even if you would like him or her to be different. You do not have to justify what you perceive or apologize. The more honest your answers, the clearer the picture, and the person will get most benefit from the exercise.

You have to say whether you agree or disagree with each statement for the way the person truly is, not how you might want him or her to be. Think carefully about how the person normally thinks, behaves and feels. For example, look at the statement that appears immediately below:

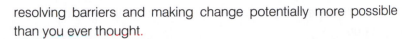

	How he or she is					
	Agree				Disagree	
	1	2	3	4	5	6
Bright and attentive	O	O	O	O	O	O

The scale is to help you put down what you think is true. You have to cross through or tick the circle that describes the person. This is what the circles mean:

1 Definitely agree.

2 Agree, but less strongly.

3 On balance, tend to agree.

4 On balance, tend to disagree.

5 Tend to disagree.

6 Definitely disagree.

For each statement, cross through or tick the circle that is most true.

Questionnaire – how the person is						
	How he or she is					
	Agree				Disagree	
	1	2	3	4	5	6
1. Prepared to take chances	O	O	O	O	O	O
2. Worries about people	O	O	O	O	O	O
3. Enjoys being alone	O	O	O	O	O	O
4. Listens more than speaks	O	O	O	O	O	O
5. Rarely feels tired	O	O	O	O	O	O
6. Has original views	O	O	O	O	O	O
7. Cautious about changes	O	O	O	O	O	O
8. Unemotional	O	O	O	O	O	O
9. Seeks people to join	O	O	O	O	O	O
10. Likes to be in charge	O	O	O	O	O	O
11. Sometimes feels weak	O	O	O	O	O	O
12. Distrusts his or her imagination	O	O	O	O	O	O
13. Easily distracted	O	O	O	O	O	O
14. Upset by cruel remarks	O	O	O	O	O	O
15. Bored at social events	O	O	O	O	O	O
16. Does not argue	O	O	O	O	O	O
17. More energy than most	O	O	O	O	O	O
18. Comes up with ideas	O	O	O	O	O	O
19. Careful	O	O	O	O	O	O
20. Takes tough decisions	O	O	O	O	O	O
21. Included by others	O	O	O	O	O	O
22. Usually takes command	O	O	O	O	O	O
23. Occasionally needs to rest	O	O	O	O	O	O

Questionnaire – how the person is						
	How he or she is					
	Agree				Disagree	
	1	2	3	4	5	6
24. Holds traditional views	O	O	O	O	O	O
25. Bored by routine	O	O	O	O	O	O
26. Sensitive to criticism	O	O	O	O	O	O
27. Socializes only if he or she has to	O	O	O	O	O	O
28. Accepts others' decisions	O	O	O	O	O	O
29. Highly active	O	O	O	O	O	O
30. Has invented something	O	O	O	O	O	O
31. Does not like uncertainty	O	O	O	O	O	O
32. Sticks to facts	O	O	O	O	O	O
33. Includes others	O	O	O	O	O	O
34. Influences people	O	O	O	O	O	O
35. Cannot always cope	O	O	O	O	O	O
36. Wary of new ideas	O	O	O	O	O	O
37. Likes risks	O	O	O	O	O	O
38. A 'soft-hearted' type	O	O	O	O	O	O
39. Likes own company	O	O	O	O	O	O
40. Lets others take the lead	O	O	O	O	O	O
41. Always busy	O	O	O	O	O	O
42. Improves the way things work	O	O	O	O	O	O
43. Properly finishes things off	O	O	O	O	O	O
44. Strong-willed	O	O	O	O	O	O
45. Usually with someone	O	O	O	O	O	O
46. Likes his or her orders followed	O	O	O	O	O	O
47. Lacks determination	O	O	O	O	O	O
48. Conventionally minded	O	O	O	O	O	O

Questionnaire – how the person is						
	How he or she is					
	Agree				Disagree	
	1	2	3	4	5	6
49. Changes his or her mind rapidly	O	O	O	O	O	O
50. Avoids upsetting others	O	O	O	O	O	O
51. Works best alone	O	O	O	O	O	O
52. Tends to hold back	O	O	O	O	O	O
53. Works in his or her leisure time	O	O	O	O	O	O
54. Gets flashes of inspiration	O	O	O	O	O	O
55. Likes things to stay the same	O	O	O	O	O	O
56. Deals firmly with people	O	O	O	O	O	O
57. Tries to get to know people	O	O	O	O	O	O
58. Takes control of people	O	O	O	O	O	O
59. Sometimes wants to give up	O	O	O	O	O	O
60. Fearful of change	O	O	O	O	O	O

Mark the results in the same way as for the earlier questionnaire.

In the six personality factors chart below, mark the respondent's perception of you – 'How he or she is' – with a tick and draw a line to connect the points. Mark in your own scores too – 'How I am' with a cross and 'How I want to be' with a circle.

Six personality factors chart

How I am perceived by..

1   Casual

Cautious   Impulsive

   0   1   2   3   4   5   –   6   7   8   9   10

2   Tough

Soft   Tough

| 0 | 1 | 2 | 3 | 4 | 5 | – | 6 | 7 | 8 | 9 | 10 |

3   Independent

Sociable   Detached

| 0 | 1 | 2 | 3 | 4 | 5 | – | 6 | 7 | 8 | 9 | 10 |

4   Controlling

Unassuming   Authoritative

| 0 | 1 | 2 | 3 | 4 | 5 | – | 6 | 7 | 8 | 9 | 10 |

5   Energetic

Passive   Active

| 0 | 1 | 2 | 3 | 4 | 5 | – | 6 | 7 | 8 | 9 | 10 |

6   Creative

Conservative   Innovative

| 0 | 1 | 2 | 3 | 4 | 5 | – | 6 | 7 | 8 | 9 | 10 |

Example questions arising from the exercise:

Does the person see you the way you perceive yourself?

....

Why are his or her perceptions different?

....

What does this mean for the way you relate or work together?

....

Does the person want you to change in the ways you want?

....

Does the person think you limit yourself?

. . . .

How will your relationship be different after this exercise?

. . . .

What action are you going to take now?

. . . .

By when?

. . . .

Based on your findings in the action plan you completed earlier, amended by any feedback in the last exercise, you may now choose to:

- go ahead and implement any changes that you intend to make;

- seek the support of a coach or counsellor to discuss your findings and help you make these changes;

- keep this record of your intended actions, to carry forward and take into account when working through the life balance exercises in Chapter 3.

What do you want to do?

This chapter investigates what sort of work will motivate you and how your behaviour will affect the work you do. You can interpret your results from the career development profile, a questionnaire about your career, and also analyse any conflicts you may have about different types of work. You can use your findings to work through career development and monitoring exercises.

Career development profile (CDP)

This test assists you in seeking a career, changing your career or how to become more fulfilled in your current one.

Instructions

This questionnaire looks at you and the work you do or might do. It will ask what you feel about many different types of work, as well as behaviours that are important at work. It is not concerned with the level of work you might do, for example whether you are qualified to work in a professional or managerial role, but more with the basic type of work that suits you.

There are no right or wrong answers. No two people ever feel quite the same way, so it is your own feelings that count.

In the example given below, you can see that there are two statements and a key word. You have to choose the statement that, as far as you are concerned, goes better with that word.

Example: successful

a.   Collecting money for charity   G

b.   Running a youth group   <u>M</u>

You choose the statement that goes better with the key word for you and then mark your choice. Either tick or underline the 'G' or the 'M' to show which statement is better for you. At this stage, do not be concerned about what 'G' or 'M' or any other letters mean, as their purpose will be explained later. Always mark one of each pair.

In the example shown, the answer 'M' has been underlined. Thus running a youth group went with 'successful' for this person. Someone else might prefer 'G'.

Part 1: successful

In this first part of the questionnaire you are asked to think about the key word 'successful'. Being successful is generally thought to mean doing well in life, achieving your purpose and getting a position where others regard you as being a success.

For each question think about the word 'successful' and about the pair of statements. In your opinion, which statement goes better with the word 'successful'? Underline or circle the letter to the right of the statement that goes better with the word 'successful'. Do not answer in the way you think you ought to feel. Please answer naturally in the way you would usually feel about the statements.

Do not worry about whether you are actually qualified to do the kind of activity in the statement. What is wanted is simply whether you would feel more successful with one of the statements rather than the other.

Successful

1 a. Assist scientists working in research.   0
   b. Play a musical instrument as a soloist or in a musical group.   I

2 a. Make or repair wooden furniture.   P
   b. Research into the composition or origin of ancient rocks.   0

3 a. Sell interesting goods in a shop or by other means.   E
   b. Work with your hands and machinery in harvesting crops.   P

4 a. Answer questions without any preparation.   BB
   b. Have time to get well prepared for questions.   CM

5 a. Be expected to be talking with others all the time.   BB
   b. Be able to cut yourself off from others.   GI

6 a. Influence strongly how things are done.   BB
   b. Go along with what the majority or your superiors decide.   PA

7 a. Teach privately one person or a small group.   S
   b. Research into atomic particles.   0

8 a. Create settings for film or theatre productions.   I
   b. Negotiate with clients in buying and selling property.   E

9 a. Arrange social activities for young people.   S
   b. Interest people in a new product by demonstrating how it is   E
       used.

10 a. Be always taking on new and difficult things.   BB
   b. Be able to work with things no one else likes.   CM

11 a. Advise on the legal and financial aspects of a business   A
       problem.
   b. Move soil or vegetation to construct or improve the   P
       landscape.

12 a. Investigate financial records or advise on accounting matters.   A
   b. Help families who are in difficulty.   S

13 a. Research into bacteria.   0
   b. Represent the views of others as a politician.   E

14 a. Use mathematics to solve scientific, engineering and other problems.   O

      b. Make sure a company's operation is legally and financially correct.   A

15 a. Design or illustrate for technical products.   I

      b. Estimate the value of property, goods or livestock.   A

16 a. Plan and organize the resources of a large hotel.   E

      b. Drive passenger or goods vehicles.   P

17 a. See what needs to be corrected in motor vehicles.   P

      b. Help people to overcome or reduce speech defects or disorders.   S

18 a. Work underwater in a diving suit to make inspections and repairs.   P

      b. Take charge of business cash, make payments and keep records.   A

19 a. Organize and direct advertising campaigns.   E

      b. Collect and index information.   A

20 a. Put out dangerous fires or advise on fire hazards.   P

      b. Write slogans or copy for advertisements.   I

21 a. Shape, fit and assemble metal parts for tools, gauges or fixtures.   P

      b. Advise on technical matters involving computers.   O

22 a. Sing as a soloist or as a member of a vocal group.   I

      b. Repair articles of precious metal.   P

23 a. Raise money from banks to start a new business.   E

      b. Be responsible for staff recruitment and employment conditions.   S

24 a. Undertake work concerned with the personal welfare of employees.   S

      b. Obtain quotations on costs from suppliers of goods or materials.   A

25 a. Organize the running of a residential home for children.   S

      b. Look after animals.   P

26	a.	Let others who have stronger feelings make decisions.	PA
	b.	Have others always look to you to make decisions on their behalf.	BB
27	a.	Look after or teach infants.	S
	b.	Collect information and report on items of current interest.	I
28	a.	Investigate and treat diseases and disorders.	O
	b.	Analyse work methods to improve effectiveness and efficiency.	A
29	a.	Create pictures, designs or visual compositions.	I
	b.	Advise on economic matters.	A
30	a.	Buy goods from various sources for resale through shops.	E
	b.	Keep and balance a set of day-to-day financial accounts.	A
31	a.	Avoid situations of unnecessary risk.	CM
	b.	Take risks if there is a chance of achieving more.	BB
32	a.	Meet many new people.	BB
	b.	Meet only people you know.	GI
33	a.	Consider everyone's ideas equally with your own.	PA
	b.	Persuade others to accept your ideas.	BB
34	a.	Help people to obtain employment.	S
	b.	Act in dramatic productions.	I
35	a.	Prepare programs for computers.	O
	b.	Organize the running of a team engaged in competitive sport.	E
36	a.	Conduct tourists.	E
	b.	Photograph items for publication.	I
37	a.	Work by yourself or with just one or two others.	GI
	b.	Work with a large group.	BB
38	a.	Be slow in order to prevent mistakes.	CM
	b.	Be quick in order to get a lot done even if there are some mistakes.	BB
39	a.	Be able to discuss problems with others.	BB
	b.	Be expected to solve problems on your own.	GI
40	a.	Look after children in a nursery, home or hospital.	S
	b.	Investigate mental processes of human beings and animals.	O

41	a.	Analyse chemicals.	0
	b.	Write books or articles.	I
42	a.	Take on responsibility for difficult decisions.	BB
	b.	Share decisions with others.	PA

Part 2: contented

In this part of the questionnaire you are to make your answers in just the same way, but the key word to think about this time is 'contented'.

For many people the word 'contented' usually means something different from 'successful'. 'Contented' is generally thought to mean: satisfied, accepting, achieving your own personal goals and being in a state where you are happy with things as they are. Think for a moment about what being contented means for you.

Again, for each question think about the word 'contented' and about the pair of statements. Which statement in your opinion goes better with the word 'contented'? Mark your answer on the answer sheet.

Do not spend too long thinking about any question. Do not answer as you think you ought to feel. Do not worry whether you are actually qualified or able to do the kind of activity in the statement.

When you are ready and have an idea of what 'contented' means to you please continue.

Contented

43	a.	Investigate mental processes and behaviour.	0
	b.	Play a musical instrument as a soloist or in a musical group.	I
44	a.	Repair articles of precious metal.	P
	b.	Advise on technical matters involving computers.	0
45	a.	Negotiate with clients in buying and selling property.	E
	b.	Work with your hands and machinery in harvesting crops.	P
46	a.	Stay in one place.	CM
	b.	Travel a lot.	BB

47	a.	Join in with others a lot.	BB
	b.	Be able to separate yourself from others when you wish.	GI
48	a.	Have as much control of others as they have of you.	PA
	b.	Control what others do.	BB
49	a.	Help people overcome speech defects or disorders.	S
	b.	Prepare programs for computers.	O
50	a.	Create settings for films or theatre productions.	I
	b.	Sell interesting goods in a shop or by other means.	E
51	a.	Arrange social activities for young people.	S
	b.	Plan and organize the resources of a large hotel.	E
52	a.	Repeat what you do in order to become better at it.	CM
	b.	Avoid doing the same thing twice.	BB
53	a.	Advise on financial accounting methods.	A
	b.	Drive passenger or goods vehicles.	P
54	a.	Organize the running of a residential home for children.	S
	b.	Advise on economic matters.	A
55	a.	Analyse chemicals.	O
	b.	Represent the views of others as a politician.	E
56	a.	Use mathematics to solve scientific, engineering and other problems.	O
	b.	Obtain quotations on costs from suppliers of goods or materials.	A
57	a.	Write slogans or copy for advertisements.	I
	b.	Estimate the value of property, goods or livestock.	A
58	a.	Raise money from banks to start a new business.	E
	b.	Move soil or vegetation to construct or improve the landscape.	P
59	a.	Look after animals.	P
	b.	Help families who are in difficulty.	S
60	a.	Work underwater in a diving suit to make inspections and repairs.	P
	b.	Advise clients on the legal and financial aspects of business.	A

61 a. Organize the running of a team engaged in competitive sport.   E

      b. Make sure a company's operation is legally and financially correct.   A

62 a. Put out dangerous fires or advise on fire hazards.   P

      b. Design or illustrate for technical products.   I

63 a. Make or repair wooden furniture.   P

      b. Investigate and treat diseases and disorders.   O

64 a. Sing as a soloist or as a member of a vocal group.   I

      b. Shape, fit and assemble metal parts for tools, gauges or fixtures.   P

65 a. Interest people in a new product by demonstrating how it is used.   E

      b. Look after children in a nursery, home or hospital.   S

66 a. Help school people to obtain employment.   S

      b. Collect and index information.   A

67 a. Undertake work concerned with the personal welfare of employees.   S

      b. See what needs to be corrected in motor vehicles.   P

68 a. Share power with everyone else.   PA

      b. Have more power than others.   BB

69 a. Teach privately one person or a small group.   S

      b. Collect information and report on items of current interest.   I

70 a. Research into the composition or origins of ancient rocks.   O

      b. Analyse work methods in order to improve efficiency.   A

71 a. Create pictures, designs or visual compositions.   I

      b. Keep and balance a set of day-to-day financial accounts.   A

72 a. Organize and direct advertising campaigns.   E

      b. Make payments and maintain records in a business.   A

73 a. Make things up as you go along.   BB

      b. Plan carefully what you want to do.   CM

74	a.	Work with others around you.	BB
	b.	Work by yourself for a lot of the time.	GI
75	a.	Be in a position where others have to listen to you.	BB
	b.	Have your opinion regarded equally with those of others.	PA
76	a.	Be responsible for staff recruitment and employment conditions.	S
	b.	Photograph items for publication.	I
77	a.	Assist scientists working in research.	O
	b.	Buy goods from various sources for resale through shops.	E
78	a.	Conduct tourists.	E
	b.	Act in dramatic productions.	I
79	a.	Usually work by yourself and in your own way.	GI
	b.	Be part of a work group, project group or team.	BB
80	a.	Get the best from what there is and by avoiding waste.	CM
	b.	Take a chance on doing things in completely new ways.	BB
81	a.	Always be included in a group.	BB
	b.	Be included in groups occasionally.	GI
82	a.	Look after or teach infants.	S
	b.	Research into atomic particles.	O
83	a.	Research into bacteria.	O
	b.	Write books, plays, poems or essays.	I
84	a.	Allow others to have authority over you.	PA
	b.	Make sure you have authority over everybody else.	BB

Marking

In Part 1, count up the number of times you have circled or underlined the letter 'I'. Write the number of times in the box in the table below under the column for 'I' and the row for 'Successful'. Do the same with the other letters or pairs of letters. Repeat with Part 2, placing the scores in the table in the row for 'Contented'. Add the scores to form totals.

Table of scores									
	I	O	E	A	P	S	CM	GI	PA
Successful									
Contented									
Total									

Results chart

Transfer your results to the career motivation chart below, which will make them easier to interpret.

Taking first of all the score you have in the 'I–Successful' box, draw a line from the left of the chart, '0' score to the number representing your score. Mark the point with a cross. Then from this point continue the line by adding your 'I–Contented' score, resulting in a line showing your total score. Mark this point on the graph with a circle. You now have the two parts of your total score in the graph.

Do the same with all your scores.

Career motivation chart

Interest factors

I Intuitive

0 1 2 3 4 5 6 7 8 9 10 11 12 13 14 15 16 17 18 19 20

O Objective

0 1 2 3 4 5 6 7 8 9 10 11 12 13 14 15 16 17 18 19 20

E Enterprising

0 1 2 3 4 5 6 7 8 9 10 11 12 13 14 15 16 17 18 19 20

A Administrative

0 1 2 3 4 5 6 7 8 9 10 11 12 13 14 15 16 17 18 19 20

P Practical

0 1 2 3 4 5 6 7 8 9 10 11 12 13 14 15 16 17 18 19 20

S Social

0 1 2 3 4 5 6 7 8 9 10 11 12 13 14 15 16 17 18 19 20

Behavior factors graph

Changing				CM			Maintaining	
0	1	2	3	4	5	6 ·	7	8

Group				GI			Independent	
0	1	2	3	4	5	6	7	8

Power				PA			Accepting	
0	1	2	3	4	5	6	7	8

Making sense of your chart

The interest factors in your chart above indicate the types of work that most (and least) appeal to you. High scores to the right of the chart are related to types of work that appeal to you most, and low scores to the left of the chart relate to those jobs that have little or no appeal for you.

Your behavioural styles are also shown in the chart. On each factor, your behaviour will range somewhere from one extreme to the other. Nowhere along this range is it suggested that there is any 'best' or 'ideal' place to be; it just indicates different ways you typically perform or relate to others. Your behavioural style will also influence the types of work activity best suited to you.

The analysis that follows will give some examples of the type of work that may appeal to you most. These are only examples for you to think about, since it is not possible to list every job. The analysis does not intend to tell you exactly what you should do, only to act as a guide.

Look first at your total scores and see what your strongest preferences are. Then look at the options below that correspond with your preferences. Suggestions are also given for second or even third choice of work type. This is because people often want to combine different kinds of work activity in their job, and most jobs cover more than one type of work.

When you find a job that appeals, you should ask yourself questions such as 'Am I qualified to do it?' 'What further qualifications would I need?' 'Do I have the right experience?' 'If not, how do I get it?'

You also need to think about any major differences between your scores for 'contented' and 'successful', so the analysis will also point out any areas where you seem to be uncertain at the moment. Once you have become clearer about the *type* of work you want, you can find out more from the library or from careers advisers.

The work development exercises at the end of this chapter can also help you explore your career options further.

Interest factors

I	Intuitive	Creative activities allowing some artistic or imaginative expression.
O	Objective	Activities that are primarily scientific and logical.
E	Enterprising	Activities that are business winning and developing.
A	Administrative	Activities related to dealing with organizational information, including accounts.
P	Practical	Activities where there is a contact with materials or that are active, possibly outdoors.
S	Social	Activities related to welfare and training.

Behavioural factors

CM	Changing or maintaining	The lower the score on this factor, the more likely it is that you will want to have a changing and adventurous environment, with a personal involvement in risk taking or in a risk-orientated environment. The higher the score, the more emphasis is put on maintaining existing systems and working in a persevering, disciplined and controlled way.

GI	Group member or independent	The lower the score, the more likely it is that you will want to be involved as a member of a team. This does not mean necessarily that you are a leader or extrovert, but that you enjoy group membership. The higher the score, the more likely it is that you prefer not to be included, either because of a reserved temperament or because you prefer emotional detachment.
PA	Power orientated or accepting temperament	The lower the score on this factor, the more likely it is that you enjoy power or working in a situation where responsibilities are clearly understood and authority is respected. With a higher score you are likely to be more tolerant of control by others and be supportive in relationships.

No value judgement pertains to any of the above dimensions. They are polar dimensions, and all may be effective and relevant depending upon different circumstances and how you choose to be.

Are you more successful or contented?

Within each factor are two sub-scores, which combine to give a total score. The sub-scores permit investigation of discrepancies between what you say you want, insofar as you allow yourself to be influenced by pressures from influences outside yourself, and what you would like to achieve if such influences were removed.

What you experience as 'outside pressures' may or may not be real, but many people do, for various reasons, have conflicts about what work they want to do. It is useful to attempt to establish what these are as the best way of resolving them.

Single work interest preferences

Choose one of the following that corresponds to any distinct preference shown in your results.

Intuitive

You prefer work that involves imagination, creativity and expression. This doesn't mean that you have to be interested in art or literature – though you might be. It means that you enjoy creating new things or expressing yourself in some way. For instance, sales representatives often score highly on this factor, since they tend to enjoy opportunities for using their initiative, which gives them a sense of freedom. Success in intuitive or creative types of work often depends upon raw talent or academic qualifications.

Intuitive careers could include:

- Literary:
  - barrister;
  - solicitor;
  - librarian;
  - archivist;
  - correspondent;
  - journalist;
  - reporter;
  - translator;
  - author;
  - scriptwriter;
  - critic;
  - editor;
  - copywriter;
  - publicity officer;
  - interpreter.

- Art:
  - architect;
  - photographer;
  - designer (technical illustration, interior design, stage design, graphics, fashion);
  - artist;
  - commercial artist;
  - sculptor;
  - landscape designer;
  - florist.
- Music and entertainment:
  - music teacher;
  - instrumentalist;
  - session musician;
  - choreographer;
  - actor;
  - singer;
  - dancer;
  - entertainer;
  - model;
  - stage manager;
  - theatre technician.

Objective

Objective areas of work generally involve research and analysis, and a liking for acquiring knowledge and for logic and deduction. It suits people who are intellectually curious. You probably enjoy analytical or statistical subjects and would like a research-oriented type of job. There are also many occupations that, whilst not scientific, still require a similar objective or experimental approach.

Objective careers could include:

● Science:
  - biological scientist;
  - biochemist;
  - chemist;
  - geologist;
  - physicist;
  - mathematical scientist;
  - forensic scientist;
  - laboratory technician.

● Engineering and technology:
  - metallurgy;
  - materials;
  - fuels;
  - synthetics;
  - paper/wood;
  - print;
  - textiles;
  - food;
  - engineering (mechanical, agricultural, automotive, chemical, civil, building and construction, electrical/electronic, production, marine, aeronautical).

● Scientific applications:
  - medical research;
  - hospital physicist;
  - information scientist;
  - psychologist;
  - dietitian;
  - radiographer;

- systems analyst;

- patents work;

- surgeon;

- technical author;

- programmer;

- process description writer.

Enterprising

These areas of work often indicate material ambition, often combined with an interest in management. You probably would like to organize people and make decisions for them. Often people who score highly on this factor would like to run their own business. Enterprising people often measure their success by how much money they earn or the status of their job. Success in this area of work often depends on qualifications, plus personal qualities such as flair and initiative. The essential requirement in this area of work is the will to succeed.

Enterprising careers could include:

- Politics:
  - government;
  - political agent;
  - charity organization.

- Sport:
  - sportsperson;
  - team manager.

- Property:
  - estate agent;
  - negotiator;
  - auctioneer.

- Media:
  - publisher;
  - advertising;

- account executive;
- film producer;
- stage manager;
- road manager.

● Service:
  - solicitor;
  - entrepreneur;
  - buyer;
  - shop manager;
  - demonstrator;
  - consultant;
  - own business;
  - broking;
  - marketing;
  - sales.

Administrative

Administrative areas of work indicate an interest in finance or office administration, ie the running of a business or company. The work often appeals to people who like to be orderly and methodical, but in a commercial or administrative setting rather than a scientific one. Administration is a work activity that increasingly requires people-related skills or technical skills such as computer literacy. Nevertheless, the most important thing is to have some contact with financial, legal or commercial types of work.

Administrative careers could include:

● Commerce:
  - company solicitor;
  - actuary;
  - accountant (audit, taxation, company valuer);

- banking;
- bookkeeper;
- cashier;
- insurance.

● Administration:

- chartered secretary;
- office manager;
- personnel officer;
- stock control manager;
- record keeper (medical, library, etc);
- wages;
- rating and evaluation;
- planning;
- housing.

● Management services:

- economist;
- systems analyst;
- organization and methods;
- statistician;
- safety;
- market research.

● Industry:

- purchasing;
- wholesale;
- distribution;
- broking;
- transport;
- progress chasing.

Practical

Practical areas of work indicate a desire to be outdoors and active, rather than office bound. They can also indicate a liking to be involved with materials and products in an active and hands-on way, where the emphasis is on doing. People who score highly on 'practical' often enjoy being able physically to touch materials and make things. Therefore technical or craft activities may have some appeal. If the idea of making things yourself does not appeal, you may still enjoy working in an environment that allows you to be physically active or have contact with processes or equipment.

Practical careers could include:

- Security:
  - fire service;
  - coastguard;
  - armed forces;
  - diving;
  - police;
  - ambulance;
  - security/inspection.
- Transport:
  - waterways;
  - road services;
  - rail;
  - driving;
  - Merchant Navy;
  - civil aviation;
  - mechanical.
- Crafts:
  - animals;
  - agriculture;

- horticulture;
- forestry;
- fishing;
- stonemason;
- carver;
- technical;
- toolmaker;
- cabinetmaker;
- gunsmith;
- silversmith;
- country crafts;
- building crafts (bricklayer, carpenter/joiner, floor layer, painter/decorator, glazier, plasterer, plumber, roofer, scaffolder, wall and floor tiler);
- construction operator;
- oil drilling;
- catering.

- Services:
  - wholesale;
  - sales;
  - hotel;
  - recreation (leisure centre, sports centre, club);
  - property (surveying, landscaping);
  - engineering;
  - repair and maintenance.

Social

A high 'social' score shows that you like to assist in the well-being or development of others. In the public sector, this could involve social work, teaching, medical work or welfare-related jobs. In industry and commerce it is more likely to involve jobs connected with training and developing people. Many careers of this type require a great deal of training, as well as natural skills in dealing with, and caring for, others. Personal judgement and dedication are usually required in such jobs.

Social careers could include:

- Welfare:
    - teacher;
    - psychologist;
    - social worker;
    - nurse (geriatric, psychiatric, children, district, industrial);
    - therapist (speech, art, music, drama);
    - nursery nurse;
    - youth club leader;
    - residential care;
    - counsellor;
    - probation officer;
    - careers officer.

- Medical:
    - general practitioner;
    - dentist;
    - optician;
    - orthopaedist;
    - chiropodist;
    - physiotherapist;
    - osteopath;
    - audiologist;
    - dental auxiliary;
    - dental hygienist;
    - nurse;

- dietician;
- remedial gymnast;
- occupational therapist.

- Services:
  - catering;
  - training;
  - secretarial;
  - hairdressing;
  - travel courier;
  - retail management;
  - hospital management;
  - reception;
  - hospital and social administration;
  - institutional management;
  - beauty culture;
  - personnel work;
  - selling (through media, telephone, representative, agent).

Combined work interest preferences

Look below if you have two strong areas of work preference. They do not need to be equal, but stand out so that it looks as though you would be attracted by both areas of work.

Intuitive and social

Work that is both intuitive and social requires interest and ability in some form of art and a willingness to care for others. Therefore these types of job often demand patience and an ability to put the feelings of others first. Much of this type of work is done on a part-time or voluntary basis.

Often art has to take second place to the social side of the job, being used instead as a means for helping others rather than an end in itself. For example, teachers in schools for the mentally handicapped may be involved in painting, basketwork, sculpture and so on as part of their teaching duties.

If you prefer to use words and ideas rather than art in order to help people, then you may, for example, prefer to pass on ideas to others, helping them to learn or understand things more clearly. Most jobs in this area therefore have a connection with teaching, but there are also career possibilities in some areas connected with therapy.

Intuitive/social careers could include:

- occupational therapist;
- language teacher;
- speech therapist;
- personal skills training;
- therapies;
- nursery teacher;
- interviewer;
- liberal studies teacher;
- training officer;
- art/music therapist.

Intuitive and enterprising

Work that is both intuitive and enterprising tends to have challenge and variety. You will want to achieve and do well. You are likely to dislike routine or supportive activities and prefer those that give you a chance to make your own decisions. Jobs of this kind often require you to be 'good with words', be influential and enjoy bringing others over to your own way of thinking.

Intuitive/enterprising careers could include:

- occupational therapist;
- language teacher;
- speech therapist;
- personal skills training;
- therapies;
- interviewer;
- liberal studies teacher;
- training officer;
- art/music therapist.

Intuitive and administrative

It can be very difficult to make a living from work that is purely intuitive or creative in nature, because of either lack of outstanding talent or lack of opportunity.

Often such jobs are of the type that provide back-up or support to others, but you can combine both interests in leading roles. For example, a chef has to be aware of accounts (a restaurant has to make a profit if it is to stay in business), whilst a merchandiser who buys and sells things for profit requires an understanding of costs and creative flair. Both need strong administrative skills, and both have a variety of creative opportunities.

Intuitive/administrative careers could include:

- barrister;
- solicitor;
- company secretary;
- legal executive;
- merchandiser;

- chef;

- choreographer's assistant;

- cinema manager;

- studio assistant;

- theatre administrator;

- library assistant;

- receptionist;

- theatre box office clerk;

- wardrobe manager;

- administrator;

- entertainments officer;

- secretary.

Intuitive and practical

Work that is both intuitive and practical can be found in the arts where design is not only beautiful or attractive but useful too. Examples range from decoration, in its many forms, to product or material design and manufacture. Artistic and practical activities usually bring people with similar interests together – perhaps in some kind of workshop or studio. There is less chance of finding careers that link a liking for literary preferences (ie the written word) with practical ones. For example, how is it possible to combine writing with being active and on the go at the same time? Usually one has to stop before the other can start, or one activity (either the practical one or the creative one) may have to be left for leisure time – the activity chosen for your career being your stronger preference, or simply opportunity.

It is possible, however, to follow one of these work preferences by moving it into another setting. For example, an agricultural secretary does the same work as other secretaries but can have more opportunity to be out and about in the countryside; a printer has a mechanical and increasingly technical job (eg computerized desktop publishing, etc), although his or her initial interest may have been with words.

Intuitive/practical careers could include:

- camera person;

- cabinet maker;

- film projectionist;

- engineering pattern maker;

- jewellery maker;

- pattern cutter;

- picture framer;

- potter;

- printer;

- book binder;

- technical writer;

- gardener;

- confectioner;

- dresser;

- embroiderer;

- embalmer;

- conservation;

- horticultural.

Intuitive and objective

Jobs that combine intuitive and objective preferences are a strong indicator of intellectual leanings (ie the need to understand things). Jobs in this area need artistic and/or scientific aptitudes and skills. Although science and art are often thought to be incompatible, they can be combined in several areas of work. For example, art and engineering join forces in car styling, as well as in many other areas of engineering design. Similarly, many artists employed in the restoration of valuable old paintings need to understand chemistry and physics.

Intuitive/objective careers could include:

- anthropology;
- archaeology;
- academic;
- designer;
- cartographer;
- draughtsperson;
- medical illustrator;
- photographer;
- restorer;
- beautician;
- museum assistant.

Enterprising and social

Jobs that combine enterprising and caring types of work involve working with people and influencing what goes on around you. To do this successfully, you need to be able to get others round to your way of thinking. Jobs of this type are more often found in businesses in the private sector.

Enterprising/social careers could include:

- director of social services;
- head teacher;
- hotel manager;
- funeral director;
- retail manager;
- salesperson.

Enterprising and administrative

Jobs that combine enterprising and administrative types of work are found in banking, insurance, commerce, office administration and so on. They involve management and making business decisions, rather than a purely technical role. It is the commercial side of businesses that you will find interesting. If you gain the right technical knowledge and professional qualifications, you could get into general management.

Enterprising/administrative careers could include:

- finance director;
- tax consultant;
- bank manager;
- estate manager;
- underwriter;
- broker;
- club manager;
- insurance agent;
- office manager;

- sales administrator;
- turf accountant.

Enterprising and practical

Jobs that combine enterprising and practical types of work indicate a wish to be involved with commerce and administration – without being too confined or desk bound. You probably prefer to be on the move, rather than being stuck in one place for too long. There are a number of enterprising jobs that could let you get out and about. These types of job often relate to the land, agricultural products, property, manufacturing, and working in other ways with equipment. In such types of work it is usual to combine education with practical experience and know the value of goods, products or materials.

Enterprising/practical careers could include:

- farm manager;
- production manager;
- builder;
- accident assessor;
- auctioneer;
- demonstrator;
- estate agent;
- publican;
- transport manager;
- undertaker.

Administrative and social

Jobs that combine administrative and social types of work generally involve helping people by making sure they have what they need.

They involve administering systems that provide others with the help they need, and are therefore more 'supportive' than 'front-line' in nature. Helping people in this way is less direct and less personal than working in more active, closer relationship to those being helped – as in, for example, social work.

Administrative/social careers could include:

- principal nursing officer;

- employment officer;

- courier/local representative;

- medical secretary.

Administrative and practical

Jobs that combine administrative and practical types of work can be hard to find. Administrative work usually involves sitting at a desk in an office, and practical work usually involves being physically active and working with materials and equipment. The two seemingly fairly different types of work can however be combined in one job, for example jobs that involve field work or travelling followed by spells in the office to compile reports or accounts. Many people in such jobs view the administrative side as a 'necessary evil'. This is unlikely in your case, because of your interest in such work. However, if separation of these aspects does not appeal, you may wish to consider careers such as purchasing and estimating, where the two types of work are naturally combined.

Administrative/practical careers could include:

- work study officer;

- agricultural secretary;

- baths manager;

- builders' merchant;

- customs officer;

- manufacturing superintendent;

- office machinery engineer;

- rating officer;

- storekeeper;

- trading standards officer.

Practical and social

Jobs combining practical and social activities involve being active and helping others. Many practical skills can be used to help people, but an interest in developing people is what you really enjoy. There are many activities suited to your interest in this area of work – ranging from instruction and training to the therapeutic. People with such a work preference often reject administrative types of work, which they often see as being too desk bound. They prefer a job where they can get out and about.

Practical/social careers could include:

- occupational therapist;

- chiropodist;

- police officer;

- sports centre assistant;

- team coach;

- youth leader;

- prison officer;

- hairdresser;

- massage therapist.

Objective and social

Jobs combining objective and social activities usually involve applying scientific knowledge or other analytical techniques to help people, rather than providing them with emotional support or comfort personally. Careers in this area are mainly of an advisory or technical nature and often require that the expertise provided is impartial and detached. However, personal skills, particularly tact and understanding, are none the less required in jobs of this type. You probably enjoy, or are good at, analytical or statistical subjects, but may be too outgoing to be happy with work that doesn't involve people.

Objective/social careers could include:

- clinical psychologist;
- dentist;
- orthoptist;
- science teacher;
- social science researcher;
- nurse;
- radiographer;
- dental assistant.

Objective and enterprising

Jobs that combine objective and enterprising activities require a liking for research work that has commercial opportunity. The commercialization of scientific research is often an expensive business, and therefore opportunities in this field mainly exist in large industries. However, computer-related businesses often offer opportunities with relatively little investment being required. Since it is often difficult to find commercially minded people who have a technical and scientific background, there are many opportunities for those who have.

Objective/enterprising careers could include:

- director of private research or a scientific enterprise;
- dispensing optician;
- general chemist;
- veterinary surgeon;
- manager of a computer bureau;
- medical representative;
- technical representative.

Objective and administrative

Jobs combining objective and administrative activities involve working with facts and figures. You probably enjoy dealing with information and like to work in a structured and methodical way. To a large extent, the type of work in this area that will appeal to you will be influenced by your other work type scores. For example, look at your chart again and, if your 'social' and 'intuitive' scores are fairly low, then computer systems or system analysis in an administrative or commercial work setting may appeal to you. If your 'enterprising' score is fairly high too, then some of the leading-edge, high-tech technologies might be more appealing. If, however, your 'social' score is fairly high then some areas of training may have more appeal.

Objective/administrative careers could include:

- business systems analyst;
- computer programmer;
- economist;
- market researcher;
- operational researcher;

- statistician;

- systems analyst.

Objective and practical

Jobs combining objective and practical activities involve applying scientific theories in the real world. Scientific theory and concepts might interest you, but you need to see some real benefits or results from the work you undertake. In short, you would rather help design a bridge than work on the mathematical equations used in its design. Most jobs in this area of work will almost always involve your working with people and involve business activity. However, your main interest is with equipment and technology and their use. In such cases, there is often a desire for accompanying physical activity – so that science can be seen in relation to the environment. Most careers of this type require study and expert skills.

Objective/practical careers could include:

- agriculturalist;

- hydrologist;

- biomedical engineer;

- metallurgist;

- engineer;

- navigation officer;

- ergonomist;

- scientific instrument maker;

- geologist;

- surveyor;

- horologist;

- technologist;

- computer engineer;

- work study officer;

- environmental health officer;

- safety standards inspector;

- maintenance fitter;

- service engineer.

Your behaviour scores

Changing or maintaining

If your scores are at the 'changing' end of this spectrum you will value a fast-moving work environment, radical change and some element of risk.

If your score is at the 'maintaining' end you value a conservative, traditional approach that errs on the side of caution rather than impulse.

If your score is around the middle you do not need either of these extremes of environment to feel motivated. This is useful in that it indicates that you can react to situations in a measured and balanced manner – either quickly or slowly, as the situation demands. However, it may also indicate that you would not be satisfied by a continuing requirement to work at either extreme.

Group or independent

Individuals at the 'group' end of this spectrum need to work as part of a team in order to derive real job satisfaction. Those at the 'independent' end prefer 'solo-performer' roles with minimum group interaction.

If your score is around the middle you need neither of these extremes of environment to feel motivated, preferring instead a more balanced, flexible, middle-of-the-road approach. This can be very useful, as it allows you to move between individual and team responsibilities as the organization demands. However, it may also indicate that you would not be satisfied by a continuing requirement to work at either extreme.

Power or accepting

Individuals at the 'power' end of the spectrum are motivated by a highly ordered structure, personal authority and the need to control events and others. Those at the 'accepting' end derive satisfaction from supportive activities, providing information on which others can make decisions.

If your score is around the middle you do not need either of these extremes to enjoy work, preferring instead a more balanced, flexible, middle-of-the-road approach. This is useful, since it indicates that you can adopt a controlling position or stance when required or, conversely, one that requires you to accept direction from others. However, it may also indicate that you would not be satisfied by a continuing requirement to work at either extreme.

Areas of possible uncertainty

You may be unsure about what you really want to do. You may feel that to be successful you have to do one type of job, but to be contented or happy you have to do another. Any major differences between what you associate with 'contentment' or 'success' will be evident in your results and in your chart.

Where there are significant differences in your scores ask yourself why this should be so and what causes it.

Intuitive

Are activities involving imagination, creativity and expression seen as contributing more to contentment than to success or more to success than contentment?

Objective

Are activities involving research, analysis, logic and deduction seen as contributing more to contentment than to success or more to success than contentment?

Practical

Are physical, outdoor, hands-on activities with material contact seen as contributing more to contentment than to success or more to success than contentment?

Administrative

Are activities involving running organizations, including administration, information, finance and so on seen as contributing more to contentment than to success or more to success than contentment?

Enterprising

Are business-oriented, managerial, persuasive activities involving some risk taking seen as contributing more to contentment than to success or more to success than contentment?

Social

Are activities involving the well-being and development of others seen as contributing more to contentment than to success or more to success than contentment?

Changing vs maintaining

You may prefer caution, stability and a conventional approach but perhaps associate change, variety and a more radical or unconventional approach with success. Or you may prefer change, variety and a radical or unconventional approach, but associate caution, stability and a more conventional approach with success.

Group vs independent

You may prefer a more independent, detached, self-reliant approach, but may associate being one of the team and working with others, rather than alone, with success. Or you may associate an independent, detached, self-reliant approach with success but perhaps prefer to be one of the team, working with others, rather than alone.

Power vs accepting

You may prefer a supportive, participative and accepting approach, but perhaps associate a more controlling, authoritative and assertive approach with success. Or you may associate a supportive, participative and accepting approach with success, but perhaps prefer a more controlling, authoritative and assertive approach.

How your behaviour scores fit with work

Changing

If your score indicates this behaviour, you prefer work that involves change, challenge and variety, rather than routine work that may offer greater stability. You will not be put off by difficult tasks, which you will find a challenge, and will prefer to experiment with new ways of doing things rather than relying on old, tried-and-tested methods.

Your spontaneity, when combined with your high work-type scores, can offer further information on the type of career or role best suited to you. The following possibilities emerge. Remember, these are only examples:

- Objective and changing:
  - investigative problem solving;
  - research to find new solutions;

- systems analysis;
- logical debate;
- commercial applications, contractor or consultant.

- Practical and changing:
  - trading;
  - troubleshooting;
  - crisis management;
  - making goods to order;
  - own business;
  - sport-related activities.

- Administrative and changing:
  - corporate finance;
  - purchasing;
  - buying;
  - commercial;
  - contractual or legal advice;
  - careers in industry and the private sector.

- Enterprising and changing:
  - high-venture business activity;
  - negotiating;
  - chancing personal reputation and wealth;
  - selling;
  - demonstrating or presenting.

- Social and changing:
  - coaching;
  - training;
  - representing others;
  - overseas service;
  - own occupation (professional).

- Intuitive and changing:
  - designing or illustrating;
  - brainstorming;
  - creating new products;
  - fine art;
  - freelance work.

Maintaining

If your score indicates this behaviour, you prefer to be careful and disciplined, leaving little to chance. Working in a job that demands constant change and variety will not appeal to you, and you prob-ably prefer tried-and-tested ways of doing things. Careful people generally enjoy providing a service to others, gathering the right information before making a decision. They personally avoid making quick decisions based on insufficient facts. Your preference for being cautious by nature, when combined with your high work-type scores, can offer further information on the type of career or role best suited to you. The following possibilities emerge:

- Objective and maintaining:
  - provide expert back-up services;
  - assist front-line staff;
  - critically evaluate proposals;
  - careers in the public or academic sectors.

- Practical and maintaining:
  - obtain and utilize craft or technical skills;
  - stick with preferred type of work, once found;
  - careers in public employment.

- Administrative and maintaining:
  - office-related activities;
  - professional and technical accounting;
  - administrative systems and controls.

- Enterprising and maintaining:
  - entrepreneurial, linked with conservative planning;
  - progress business by laying solid foundations.
- Social and maintaining:
  - guaranteed employment preferred;
  - security more important than material reward;
  - often public sector employment, eg teaching, nursing, etc.
- Intuitive and maintaining:
  - design activities;
  - creating products, visual aids, presentations, etc;
  - work as a member of a company or organization.

Group

If your score indicates this behaviour, you would rather work as part of a team than alone in a solo-performer role. You see group membership as a necessary part of job satisfaction. You like teamwork. Your preference for being group oriented by nature, when combined with your high work-type scores, can offer further information on the type of career or role best suited to you. The following possibilities emerge:

- Objective and group:
  - project work;
  - survey team;
  - communication of results and information.
- Practical and group:
  - practical instruction;
  - horticulture;
  - group-related work requiring interdependence, eg product team, maintenance gang, mining, fishing, armed forces, police, etc.

- Administrative and group:
  - large office setting;
  - commercial teams;
  - shared responsibility, eg banking, insurance, etc.

- Enterprising and group:
  - negotiating team, eg industrial relations work, etc;
  - project team or new business venture;
  - management of others (leadership and delegation).

- Social and group:
  - high-level involvement with, and through, people, eg caring, counselling, training, nursing, osteopath, etc.

- Intuitive and group:
  - teamwork-related activities, eg design team, joint presentations, theatre group, involving cooperation and interpersonal skills.

Independent

If your score indicates this behaviour, you prefer to be independent. This could be because you are shy, because you like to be self-reliant, or because you find others get in the way of your own efforts. This doesn't necessarily mean that you can't mix with others if you choose. It only indicates that you prefer to be independent. Your preference for being independent by nature, when combined with your high work-type scores, can offer further information on the type of career or role best suited to you.

The following possibilities emerge:

- Objective and independent:
  - work involving things and ideas;
  - research work involving analysis and data.

- Practical and independent:
  - craft work;
  - rural work;

- skills that are not people dependent;
- investigative work;
- safety-related work.

● Administrative and independent:
  - legal/financial expert;
  - work on one's own writing reports or providing data through a computer link or network;
  - financial analysis.

● Enterprising and independent:
  - solo-performer roles, not dependent upon others;
  - broking, dealing or speculating;
  - work that does not involve people management;
  - work with goods and services.

● Social and independent:
  - provision of expert advisory services to others, eg counselling, general practitioner, psychologist, dentist, etc.

● Intuitive and independent:
  - development of own unique skills and talent;
  - work that is dependent on self-motivation.

Power

If your score indicates this behaviour, you prefer to tell others what to do and have control over people, rather than have others tell you what to do. This indicates that you prefer to work in a highly ordered structure, where you know what is expected of you and have the power you feel you need to get things done. This is the way you prefer to behave, rather than what is required by any job. Your preference for being power oriented by nature, when combined with your high work-type scores, can offer further information on the type of career or role best suited to you. The following possibilities emerge:

- Objective and power:
  - processing;
  - analysis;
  - trials work and research methods.

- Practical and power:
  - repair and maintenance;
  - security;
  - control of safety;
  - police force;
  - aviation.

- Administrative and power:
  - audit;
  - taxation;
  - valuation;
  - investigative work;
  - stock control;
  - progress chasing;
  - methods analysis.

- Enterprising and power:
  - legalistic;
  - task driven;
  - factual.

- Social and power:
  - managerial responsibility, or directive roles;
  - institutional management;
  - probation;
  - technical services, eg audiology, dentistry, etc;
  - human resources/training.

- Intuitive and power:
  - technical;
  - selling;
  - design management;
  - translation;
  - dancing;
  - library/information science.

Accepting

If your score indicates this behaviour, you prefer a supportive or a sharing role to one that involves working in a power-oriented, top-down structure. You are prepared to accept the views and decisions of others, even when these are at odds with your own views. This doesn't necessarily mean that you want always to do what others tell you, only that you value other people's point of view – perhaps to the point of putting the needs of others first. Your preference for being accepting by nature, when combined with your high work-type scores, can offer further information on the type of career or role best suited to you. The following possibilities emerge:

- Objective and accepting:
  - data analysis;
  - computer programming;
  - computer interaction.

- Practical and accepting:
  - maintenance assignments;
  - service duties, eg fire, ambulance, waterways, etc;
  - repair activities;
  - rural crafts;
  - recreation;
  - work involving animals.

- Administrative and accepting:
  - accounts work;
  - administrative support;
  - training administration;
  - housing.
- Enterprising and accepting:
  - committee work;
  - charity organizations;
  - negotiating support;
  - organizing for team leader;
  - auctioneering;
  - retail and hotel industries.
- Social and accepting:
  - personal assistance;
  - therapies;
  - reception/secretarial;
  - beauty culture;
  - voluntary work.
- Intuitive and accepting:
  - artistic design;
  - creative support, eg strategic solutions, etc;
  - illustration;
  - session musician.

Middle scores (changing-maintaining)

You are neither extreme, which can be useful, because it means that you can react to situations in balanced way – either quickly or slowly as the situation demands. However, it can also indicate that you would not be totally satisfied working in a job that needed you to work at either extreme (either too quick or too slow).

Middle scores (group-independent)

You are neither extreme, which can be very useful, since it allows you to move between individual and team responsibilities as the job demands. However, it can also indicate that you would not be totally satisfied working in a job that needed you to work at either extreme (either always being part of a team or group or always having to work on your own).

Middle scores (power-accepting)

You are neither extreme, which is useful, since it means that you can be in control when required or accept direction from others when necessary. However, it can also indicate that you would not be totally satisfied working in a job that needed you to work at either extreme (either always having to be in control or always expecting others to make decisions for you).

Career development planning

You will have your own notion of what 'job satisfaction' means to you. This, after all, is what you are after. One thing is for certain: job satisfaction cannot be imposed upon you from the outside.

Satisfaction in work, or in life for that matter, derives from your basic values. If you value something, that is to say something is important to you, then you will obtain satisfaction by involving yourself in it. If, on the other hand, you value nothing, then you will probably do nothing – or the equivalent! In other words, your values lie behind your motivation.

To derive real satisfaction from work it is important to ensure that how we spend our time doing work accords with our basic values. The career development profile (CDP) questionnaire you have completed has helped you to analyse that very area, because it has compared the relative value that you place on work and behavioural factors.

In an ideal world you would now need only to flick through the jobs listed above that have emerged from your analysis, choosing the ones that most adequately meet all of your work and behavioural factor preferences, apply for them and get the job!

Unfortunately, we live in the real world, which is often far from ideal. In the real world, commercial and other organizations expect us to possess certain skills, abilities and aptitudes, as well as relevant experience. Sometimes they demand the 'right' attitude – in line with their values. After all, whilst every employer would presumably prefer employees who are motivated, they are unlikely to offer someone a job solely on the basis that the individual likes doing it! Overall performance, which is what the average employer is most interested in, is dependent upon all of these other factors, as well as upon motivation. This is where these development planning exercises come in.

The following exercises have been designed to enable you to work through the most important challenges in getting a job in such a way as to balance them against your work and behavioural preferences, as highlighted by your CDP results. The final output should be a meaningful action plan.

Applying the CDP results to focus your career choices

In the following pages you can refine the range of possible job choices into a manageable list that focuses on your strongest motivators. Do not worry about your lack of experience or your skill gaps at this stage. These will be considered later. It is important that you decide what you really want to do before reducing your options by self-perceived limitations.

Note that this section may take several days, even weeks, as you find out about different types of jobs from various sources, such as books, careers advisers or others. It is important not to rush this part of your programme.

Exercise 1

Carefully look back and review your high work factor and combined high work factor preferences from your CDP results. Now examine the lists of career possibilities suggested by these factors. Which ones appeal to you? Write those down in the space provided below. Do the narrative and/or the jobs listed suggest any other types of job that do not actually appear? (Remember that the lists are only examples, and are directional rather than prescriptive.) Add any others you can think of to your list.

Now turn to the pages in your CDP results that describe your behavioural factor preferences. In what way or ways might these comments modify your list? Are there any jobs that clearly cannot satisfy your typical behaviours? If so, strike them from your list. Do the comments suggest other jobs that you had not previously thought of? If so, add these to your list.

Your skills or aptitudes portfolio

Instead of 'skill' or 'aptitude', the term 'competence' is widely used by organizations. It means those aptitudes that are thought to be required to perform effectively in a certain job. In this section, you assess your personal and interpersonal skills or aptitudes against a fairly comprehensive set of competences. You can also compare your self-assessment with an assessment carried out by someone who knows you well – perhaps your boss, a subordinate, a work colleague or a friend.

Ability/competence checklist

Below, you will find an ability or competence checklist comprising 41 abilities grouped into eight classes. To the right of the ability definitions there are five boxes headed E, H, M, L and 0. This allows the checklist to be used as a questionnaire by placing a tick indicating your skill level in the appropriate box alongside each ability. This is what the letters mean:

E   Exceptional level of skill

H   High level of skill

M   Medium /average level of skill

L   Low level of skill

0   No skill

For example, if you feel that you have an exceptionally high ability to persevere and see things through to the end, but are absolutely useless with detail, you would tick box E against competence number 1 and box 0 against competence number 2.

Now work through the checklist, scoring yourself honestly on each of the 41 competences.

You will notice that there are additional blank rows (42 to 45) for competences. This is to allow you to add any other relevant strengths, ie where you rate yourself 'H' or 'E'. These may be related to a hobby or leisure pursuit. Think for a while of all the things that you are pretty good at – in the home, at evening classes, during leisure hours – and add these as appropriate.

Exercise 2a

Ability/competence checklist					
Self-management:	E	H	M	L	0
1. Perseverance Maintaining output, keeping going despite obstacles; resilient; energetic.					
2. Detail awareness Covers small as well as large aspects of the job.					
3. Flexibility Adaptable to changes in tasks and people.					
4. Initiative Self-motivated; productive; little need for direct guidance from others.					
5. Time management Plans, organizes own time effectively.					
Management:	E	H	M	L	0
6. Control Disciplined and orderly. Balanced, reasonable approach. Structured, consistent.					
7. Delegation Asks for help in reasonable, fair way. States fairly what can or cannot be done.					
8. Organization Coordinates activities of others to achieve interdependent goals.					

9. Planning
  i. Understands sequence of actions to achieve goals.
  ii. Identifies long-term needs and organizes their
    fulfilment.					

10. Treatment of others Sees people as individuals. Has regard for them. Has a helpful attitude to all types of people.					
11. Leadership Ensures that all views are taken into account. Brings quieter members into discussions. Maintains balance.					

Ability/competence checklist					
Analytical:	E	H	M	L	0
12. Problem analysis Identifies reasons from facts.					
13. Decision making Makes rational and logical judgements. Uses critical thinking skills.					
14. Financial analysis Understands and accurately interprets financial data.					
15. Critical questioning Probes arguments between facts and opinions. Does not accept statements on face value.					
Communication:	E	H	M	L	0
16. Oral expression Clear and intelligible.					
17. Presentation Gets ideas and proposals across well by use in formal and informal situations.					
18. Written presentation Clear, concise, legible. Reports/letters make sense.					
19. Listening Pays attention. Acknowledges what others say.					
20. Proactive Keeps others informed without need for information being requested.					
Self-adjustment:	E	H	M	L	0
21. Stress tolerance Remains calm under pressure, possibly thrives on it.					
22. Patience Willing to wait for the fruits of labour to develop over time.					
23. Physical fitness Physically active and able.					

Ability/competence checklist					
Interpersonal:	E	H	M	L	0
24. Empathy Sensitive and aware of the feelings of others.					
25. Ice-breaking Immediate positive impact on others. Establishes and maintains rapport.					
26. Social Maintains dynamic and positive social intercourse with individuals and groups.					
27. Influential Wins others over to his or her ideas or suggestions. Persuasive. In negotiations uses objective, balanced arguments to achieve goals or compromise.					
28. Team player Sustains harmony and cooperation between group members.					
29. Networking Uses contacts to obtain required resources or information.					

Ability/competence checklist					
Entrepreneurial:	E	H	M	L	0
30. Independent Actions and direction governed by strong personal belief rather than outside influence.					
31. Risk taking Willing to risk personal finance and reputation to achieve objectives.					
32. Opportunistic Spots openings for new business or business expansion.					
33. Awareness Has insight into dynamics of environmental variables such as the economic and political climate and their impact upon the market.					
34. Vision Perceives the overall situation within which he or she frames goals.					
35. Innovative Creates or identifies with new, radical actions and solutions.					
Technical:	E	H	M	L	0
36. Driving Possesses a current driving licence.					
37. Secretarial Typing, word processing, telephone.					
38. Computer literacy Uses IT packages to improve efficiency and effectiveness of operation.					
39. Craftsmanship Able to make things. Good at DIY.					
40. Budgeting Plans take realistic costs into account. Controls budget.					
41. Professional Holds a professional qualification.					

Ability/competence checklist					
Your own list, as necessary:	E	H	M	L	0
42.					
43.					
44.					
45.					

Your skills spectrum

Your next task is to transfer your results to your skills spectrum below so that you end up with five lists of skills ranging from 'exceptional' to 'none'.

Take each of the 41 abilities/competences and place the number in the box below. So, if on number 5 you awarded yourself an 'H', place a 5 in the 'H' box. The purpose of the AR letters will be explained later. Remember, these are the ratings:

E   Exceptional level of skill

H   High level of skill

M   Medium /average level of skill

L   Low level of skill

0   No skill

AR   Assessor's rating

Exercise 2b

Your skills spectrum									
E	AR	H	AR	M	AR	L	AR	0	AR

Now you need to find someone else to score you in the 41 competences. If you are working this should, ideally, be your superior. Alternatively, an ex-boss, work peer, colleague or friend could do it. (The only problem with subordinate and, to a lesser extent, peer ratings is that they may be too kind – you need to be sure that whoever you choose will give an honest opinion!)

Ideally, your chosen assessor will not have seen your self-assessment, to prevent any bias. All you can do is to make the assessor conscious of the problem, so ask the person to be honest, not spare your feelings and not allow him- or herself to be influenced by your own ratings. Remember also to instruct your chosen assessor on how to complete the competence checklist, Exercise 2a.

Your assessor should now put his or her ratings into Exercise 2a.

When you have obtained this second opinion, transfer the results to your skills spectrum (Exercise 2b) by placing your assessor's rating (E, H, M, L or 0) in the column AR to the right of each of your five lists.

Consider and act on the results as follows:

- Where the second opinion matches or is in the column adjacent to your own rating, assume that your self-assessment is accurate.

- Where the second opinion is two or more columns to the left (ie higher) of your own rating ask yourself whether you are underestimating your own skill level in this area of competence. If necessary talk it through with your assessor to see why there is such a difference. Where the second opinion is two or more columns to the right (ie lower) of your own rating then you must seriously consider whether you are fooling yourself about your skill level. How do you compare with your peer group? It could be that your assessor has got it wrong, of course, but that could have pretty serious implications, especially if he or she is your boss! Once again you may need to talk through these differences with your assessor.

When you have completed an agreed version of your skills spectrum go on to the next section, which explains how to use the results.

Your abilities and career priority

Thinking about your personal strengths and abilities (your 'E's and 'H's, which you identified in Exercise 2), have another look at the narrative description of your work and behavioural factor preferences in your CDP analysis.

- Do you see any complementary areas?

- Are some of the things that you are good at, or know a lot about, related to your areas of interest indicated by the report?

Now, thinking again about your strengths and skills, look at the list of jobs that you selected in Exercise 1.

- Which of these appeal most?

- Do some seem more relevant to your personal skills and experience than others?

- Do some provide greater opportunity to use your skills to the full?

(If you did not seek advice on job content as part of Exercise 1 perhaps you should do so now.)

Exercise 3

In order to produce a career choice priority list (Exercise 3b below) you now need to rank your career possibilities using the paired comparisons technique (Exercise 3a).

Example of paired comparisons technique											
Career options	1 Teacher	2 Accountant	3 Dentist	4 Journalist	5 Etc	6 Etc	7	8	9	10	Total
1 Teacher		Y	Y	N							2
2 Accountant	N		N	N							0
3 Dentist	N	Y		N							1
4 Journalist	Y	Y	Y								3

Note that boxes 1/1, 2/2, 3/3 and 4/4 have not been scored. To do so would mean comparing 'teacher' to 'teacher', 'accountant' to 'accountant', etc!

To carry out Exercise 3a, follow these steps:

- Do you have more than 10 career possibilities on your list?

- If you do have more than 10, try to delete those possibilities that fit least well with your interests, abilities and experience, with the aim of reducing the list to 10 or fewer.

- List your 10 (or fewer) jobs in any order, 1–10, in the career options column on the vertical axis.

- Repeat this list in the same order on the career options row on the horizontal axis.

- Think about job number 1 on the vertical axis under the heading 'career options'. You must now compare it to every other job by working across the matrix and placing a 'Y' for 'yes' to indicate that you prefer job number 1 and an 'N' for 'no' to indicate that you prefer the alternative. For instance, in the example of paired comparisons technique given above, the individual concerned would prefer to be a teacher rather than an accountant or a dentist, but would not prefer to be a teacher rather than a journalist.

- When you have placed a Y or a N under every alternative to job 1, move down the career options column to job number 2 and again work across the matrix, placing a Y if you prefer job number 2 and an N if you prefer the alternative.

- Continue down through the career options column, comparing all jobs to every alternative until all boxes, ie 1/1 to 10/10, have been answered Y or N (ignoring the boxes with asterisks).

Exercise 3a Paired comparisons technique											
Career options	1	2	3	4	5	6	7	8	9	10	Total
1	*										
2		*									
3			*								
4				*							
5					*						
6						*					
7							*				
8								*			
9									*		
10										*	

Scoring and interpreting your results

Simply count the Ys across the matrix in respect of each option listed and place the total in the total column to the right of the matrix. In the example given above, option 1, teacher, had two Ys and therefore scored 2.

The job with the highest score is your first choice, that with the next highest is your second choice, and so on.

Career choice priority list

To complete Exercise 3b, your career choice priority list, place the highest-scoring job in row 1, the next highest in row 2, etc, until you have ranked all of your jobs.

Exercise 3b	
1	
2	
3	
4	
5	
6	
7	
8	
9	
10	

You have now arrived at the stage where you need to convert your earlier work into a concrete action plan with specific objectives and a defined route or career path, with milestone dates along the way.

Career action plan

The framework for the action plan is shown in Exercise 4 below. Firstly, reflect upon your skill gaps (or development needs); then write the job title of the job of your first choice in Box 1.

Exercise 4

BOX 1

Final career choice . . . .

. . . .

How will you confirm that opportunities exist? You may already have done this as part of your earlier deliberations. If not, you may need to consider the following routes:

- career advice or counselling;

- making enquiries at the Jobcentre;

- making enquiries at relevant professional associations;

- making enquiries at recruitment agencies;

- making enquiries with employers in your chosen field.

Now decide and list each of the routes you intend to follow in Box 2. Remember to enter the date that you will pursue each route.

BOX 2

How will I confirm that opportunities exist?
Careers adviser/counsellor Date ....
Jobcentre Date ....
Professional associations Date ....
Recruitment agencies Date ....
Employers Date ....
Job literature Date ....

What else do you need to do now?

This may have been covered by your actions in Box 2. On the other hand, you may need actually to start applying for jobs or appropriate courses. You decide, and again list the actions with dates in Box 3.

BOX 3

Write to potential employers seeking possibilities?
Date ....
Date ....
Date ....
Date ....
Date ....
Date ....
Date ....
Date ....
Date ....
Date ....
Select further development courses?
Date ....
Date ....
Date ....
Date ....
Date ....
Date ....
Date ....
Date ....
Date ....
Date ....
Date ....

What about alternative career choices?

Do you have an ideal career choice already made? If yes, move on to Box 5. If no, complete Box 4.

BOX 4

	Do I need to consider my second, third, etc choices against boxes 1 and 2 before embarking on further development needs?
2nd	
3rd	
4th	

(If there is little to choose between your first few options, or if there is a strong possibility that your first choice may not happen, perhaps because of lack of opportunities or very strong competition, etc, then complete Boxes 1–4 for as many other career choices as you feel are necessary – and take the actions!)

How will you meet your development needs?

Think about:

- Who are the people you may need to talk to? These may include people already doing this type of work.

- Could you obtain experience in this area in vocational or voluntary work?

- Could you practise or learn at home?

- Will reading help? If it will, which books do you need?

- What training courses are available?

- Are there any opportunities for sponsorship?

- Would any companies or organizations let you carry out a project for them, on an expenses-only basis if necessary, in order for you to gain experience?

How to complete Box 5

- Column 1: Decide what your development needs are, and then make a list in this column.

- Column 2: Having considered the above and any other possible relevant questions, list your specific intentions in column 2 against each development need.

- Column 3: Think about how you will be different when you have met your own specific development needs, whether it is a paper qualification, direct experience or simply a feeling of confidence you previously did not have. Write this down in column 3 against each development need.

- Column 4: Enter realistic dates for completion of your new training, reading, project work, etc. Of course, you may not be able to enter some of these dates until you have got answers to, or researched, your questions.

BOX 5: How will you meet your development needs?

Column 1	Column 2	Column 3	Column 4
Development needs?	Specific intentions?	How will I be different?	By when? (give date)

When do you aim to start your new career? Give yourself a clear target and a precise date in Box 6.

BOX 6: When am I going to start my new career?

Date . . . .

. . . .

From planning to action

Now all that remains is for you to start applying for jobs or possibly sponsorship for one of your development needs. Some pointers on this are given here.

Applying for jobs

Get help, if you need it, with advice on personal presentation, interview skills, letter writing and completing application forms. The points that follow should be treated as a checklist of absolute musts if you are to impress a potential employer in writing or in person.

Letters and applications

Through the CDP you have a good understanding of your own interests and motivations and of the types of career and work environment to which they relate. Through your self-analysis in the exercises you have a personal skills portfolio that you can explain to others. Your research has provided you with a better understanding of the content and responsibilities of the career areas in which you have shown an interest. Possibly the most important of all, you now know what you want! You must use all of these assets as follows:

● Make your written applications action oriented. Let the organization know what you are capable of!

- Tell the potential employer why you are interested in it. You have researched this area – use it!

Don't miss the opportunity to link the job on offer and the organizational environment to your work factor and behavioural preferences. If you like work that is analytical or administrative or that involves caring for others, a changing and varied environment, teamwork or whatever, let the employer know!

Most important of all, you now know what you want! You must use all of these assets in (re)designing your CV or résumé, drafting covering letters and online applications and preparing for interview, as detailed in the following paragraphs.

Curriculum vitae (CV) or résumé

A CV or résumé must:

- Present the reader with an instant image of 'who you are'.

- Illustrate your potential value to the company or organization.

- Instantly grab the attention of the reader. (The average manager takes approximately 30 seconds to scan a CV. Research suggests that he or she also decides whether to read on after scanning the first half-page!)

- Show your knowledge of the industry, sector or occupation you are targeting and show any prospective employer that you understand its needs and challenges. (But see the section on covering letters below.)

- Record what you have (personally) done or achieved rather than list your 'theoretical' role responsibilities.

- Be 'content rich' (no frills), but succinct (ideally two but no more than three pages).

- Stand up to specific questions (at interview) on each and every statement you have made.

- Use active rather than passive verbs.

- Quantify achievements, wherever possible (eg if you helped to increase sales, then from what to what and over what period). The majority of organizations like numbers!

- Make the most of all of your achievements – whether they were in employment, at school or part of a hobby.

Covering letters and online applications

It is possible and often makes good sense to tailor your CV to meet the needs of the target industry or organization. However, it is invariably desirable to send a covering letter with your CV. This is particularly important where it is not immediately obvious from your CV that you are an ideal candidate for the role.

Your covering letter should:

- Be your self-marketing tool – showing how well your skills and experience match the needs of the organization.

- Be based on research – showing your knowledge of the organization or industry and its challenges. (If it is in response to an advertisement, ring the HR manager to ask for a copy of the company accounts, job description, etc.)

- Address the stated needs (if any) of the position.

- Include your contact information.

- Tell the reader what you are seeking – an interview, meeting or telephone chat?

- Be reasonably short – a few brief but powerful paragraphs. Keep it down to a single page.

- Show your enthusiasm, but remain reasonably formal (eg address to Mr/Ms, etc unless you know the recipient personally).

Your covering letter should not:

- begin by referring to your enclosed CV;

- be addressed 'To Whom It May Concern';

- mention why you are leaving or thinking of leaving your present employment.

Job interviews

There have been many books written on preparing for and conducting yourself in an interview, but the main points to remember are covered in the following few paragraphs.

Job interviews are two-way meetings. A job interview is as much an opportunity for you to assess the organization and your potential bosses as for them to assess you. Therefore prepare your list of questions – possibly to test whether the job will really satisfy your interests and allow you to be the person you want.

Generally speaking, an interviewer will want to assess your 'fit' for the job in the following areas:

- physical make-up, appearance, etc;

- attainments and achievements;

- general intelligence and common sense;

- special relevant aptitudes such as numerical and verbal abilities, mechanical aptitude, manual dexterity, etc, depending upon the job, interests and hobbies;

- interpersonal skills, self-reliance, etc;

- personal circumstances such as family situation, willingness to relocate and other issues.

Having completed the exercises above, you should be ready for questions in these areas.

Interview questions

You can do a great deal to prepare yourself mentally for the interview by considering each of the points above and drafting (mentally, if not in writing) your best approach or response(s). For instance, how would you respond to questions such as:

- 'What key strengths would you bring to this job?' (Don't reply 'I don't really know'!)

- 'What have you achieved that makes you feel proud? How did you achieve these?'

- 'How would you deal with a poor performer?'

- 'How would you describe your management style? How do you manage your team meetings?'

- 'What do you really enjoy?'

- 'What attracts you about coming to this company?'

- 'Why should we choose you?'

- 'What are your main development needs?' (Be careful with this one – it can be another way of finding out your weaknesses!)

- 'How would this company help you to achieve your own personal career goals?'

And don't be satisfied with three- or four-word answers. These questions provide an opportunity for you to enthuse about your interests, so grab that opportunity.

Also, you can create a very favourable impression and answer some of the above questions without even opening your mouth. For example, an enthusiastic handshake suggests strong inter-personal skills; a genuine smile suggests friendliness and a sense of humour (a smile is also one of the quickest ways to reduce your nervousness!).

Other points to remember for the interview

- Confirm your intention to turn up at the required time.

- Ask for any information on the job or organization that you don't already have, eg the last annual report. (This shows a real interest and generally impresses the prospective employer.)

- Arrive in plenty of time.

- First and last interviews of the day provide the best opportunities to make an impression (ie research has shown that interviewers consistently remember the first and last interviewees of the day more clearly than any others), so if you have a choice...!

- Don't be too familiar or too informal, but...

- Smile, shake hands enthusiastically (if invited) and look the interviewer(s) in the eye from the very start. This is a great way to relax the interviewer as well as yourself. (Even though you may feel nervous, act confidently – you are simply playing the part in this game!)

- Talk frankly and completely, but briefly. Be definite in your answers. Don't mumble under your breath. Don't cover your mouth with your hand when you speak. Don't ramble!

- Don't take notes, smoke or criticize other organizations, ex-bosses, colleagues, schools, universities, lecturers or teachers – and don't name-drop!

- Be relaxed and pleasant, but above all be yourself. Although you are trying to appear confident, don't try to be someone else – you may have to live with that character for the next few years!

- Ask any questions that you have prepared, when invited. If not invited, then towards the end of the session simply say 'I have one or two questions. Would now be a good time to ask them?' (or words to that effect).

- Always thank the interviewer(s) – even if you don't feel like it – and ask him or her what happens next.

Your work and life balance

In this chapter you can complete the life balance test (LBT), which reveals how far you are truly contented with the key areas of your life. You can analyse your results to see how and in what manner you make compromises in some areas in order to cope in others. Your possible subconscious motives are brought to the surface so that you can ask clear, objective questions of yourself. Then you can work through exercises that help you to perceive your underlying motives in a logical way so that you have the means to adjust your work and life balance in the way that you want.

Life balance test (LBT)

In the same way as in Chapter 2, the words 'contented' and 'successful' are used to ask how you feel about essential aspects of your working life and your life outside work.

If you are not in employment at the moment or are considering moving to a new job, you can also complete this test for the job you would then have and how you think your life would be. Similarly, you can complete the questionnaire for 'My last job' for how your life was at that time. In these instances, the results will give you insight into matters that may concern you as to what may have been or what may be unsatisfactory during a past or future period of your life.

No two people ever feel quite the same, so there is no right or wrong answer. It is your own feelings that count.

Be clear about the basis upon which you are taking the question- naire before you start. To make this clear, you are asked to write down the occupation you have, have had or may have, together with the date to which this employment relates, in the space below:

These results are relevant to:

My occupation. . . . .

Date. . . . .

Remember, your answers should reflect your feelings about this time.

Instructions

You are given the key word 'successful' and then the key word 'con- tented'. These words have different meanings. 'Successful' means prospering, achieving your purpose and getting to that position in life where you feel you will be regarded as a success. 'Contented' means satisfied, well pleased and being in a state of contentment. Think for a moment about what 'contented' and 'successful' mean to you. You are asked to look at pairs of sentences. You have to identify in which of the two options you feel you are more success- ful. Later you will do this with the word 'contented'. You can under- line your answer, as in the example, or circle your answer if you prefer. Look at the pair below:

Example

1   I am more successful
      a.   when out playing sports   <u>S</u>
      b.   when at home watching television   H

In this case playing sports has been felt to go better with being successful. Another person would, with different feelings, have marked 'H'.

You will see that the statements are given to you many times. However, each statement is always placed with another statement in a new way. Therefore each pair of statements is different from all the other pairs.

Do not answer in the way in which you feel you ought to. That is not what is wanted. Please answer naturally in the way you feel about the statements, by underlining or circling the appropriate letter.

Begin when you are ready.

Successful

1   I am more successful
   a.   with my family life.   F
   b.   with the way I use my spare time.   L

2   I am more successful
   a.   with the way I use my spare time.   L
   b.   with the actual work I do.   N

3   I am more successful
   a.   with my income from work.   M
   b.   with being able to do as I want at work.   A

4   I am more successful
   a.   with being able to do as I want at work.   A
   b.   with the level of my position.   S

5   I am more successful
   a.   with my family life.   F
   b.   with the actual work I do.   N

6   I am more successful
   a.   with the way I use my spare time.   L
   b.   with my income from work.   M

7   I am more successful
   a.   with the actual work I do.   N
   b.   with being able to do as I want at work.   A

8 I am more successful
    a.   with my income from work.   M
    b.   with the level of my position.   S

9 I am more successful
    a.   with my family life.   F
    b.   with my income from work.   M

10 I am more successful
    a.   with being able to do as I want at work.   A
    b.   with the people I meet at work.   R

11 I am more successful
    a.   with the actual work I do.   N
    b.   with the level of my position.   S

12 I am more successful
    a.   with my income from work.   M
    b.   with the people I meet at work.   R

13 I am more successful
    a.   with the way I use my spare time.   L
    b.   with the level of my position.   S

14 I am more successful
    a.   with the actual work I do.   N
    b.   with the people I meet at work.   R

15 I am more successful
    a.   with my family life.   F
    b.   with the level of my position.   S

16 I am more successful
    a.   with the way I use my spare time.   L
    b.   with the people I meet at work.   R

17 I am more successful
    a.   with my family life.   F
    b.   with the people I meet at work.   R

18 I am more successful
    a.   with the actual work I do.   N
    b.   with my income from work.   M

19 I am more successful
    a.   with the level of my position.   S
    b.   with the people I meet at work.   R

20 I am more successful
    a.   with the way I use my spare time.   L
    b.   with being able to do as I want at work.   A

21 I am more successful
    a.   with my family life.   F
    b.   with being able to do as I want at work.   A

Now you have to think of each statement in relation to what 'contented' means to you. 'Contented' means satisfied, well pleased and in a state of contentment.

Contented

22 I am more contented
    a.   with the people I meet at work.   R
    b.   with my family life.   F

23 I am more contented
    a.   with the level of my position.   S
    b.   with my family life.   F

24 I am more contented
    a.   with the people I meet at work.   R
    b.   with the way I use my spare time.   L

25 I am more contented
    a.   with the level of my position.   S
    b.   with the way I use my spare time.   L

26 I am more contented
    a.   with the people I meet at work.   R
    b.   with the level of my position.   S

27 I am more contented
    a.   with the level of my position.   S
    b.   with the actual work I do.   N

28 I am more contented

    a.   with being able to do as I want at work.   A

    b.   with my family life.   F

29 I am more contented

    a.   with the people I meet at work.   R

    b.   with my income from work.   M

30 I am more contented

    a.   with being able to do as I want at work.   A

    b.   with the way I use my spare time.   L

31 I am more contented

    a.   with being able to do as I want at work.   A

    b.   with the actual work I do.   N

32 I am more contented

    a.   with my income from work.   M

    b.   with my family life.   F

33 I am more contented

    a.   with the people I meet at work.   R

    b.   with being able to do as I want at work.   A

34 I am more contented

    a.   with my income from work.   M

    b.   with the way I use my spare time.   L

35 I am more contented

    a.   with the level of my position.   S

    b.   with my income from work.   M

36 I am more contented

    a.   with the actual work I do.   N

    b.   with my family life.   F

37 I am more contented

    a.   with the people I meet at work.   R

    b.   with the actual work I do.   N

38 I am more contented

    a.   with the level of my position.   S

    b.   with being able to do as I want at work.   A

39   I am more contented

    a.   with being able to do as I want at work.   A

    b.   with my income from work.   M

40   I am more contented

    a.   with my income from work.   M

    b.   with the actual work I do.   N

41   I am more contented

    a.   with the actual work I do.   N

    b.   with the way I use my spare time.   L

42   I am more contented

    a.   with the way I use my spare time.   L

    b.   with my family life.   F

Scoring the questionnaire

Count the number of times you have underlined or circled each letter in the 'successful' section and then in the 'contented' section. Put the figures, together with the totals, in the chart below:

Table of results						
	R	S	A	M	N	L	F
Successful							
Contented							
Total							

Now put your scores into the life balance chart below. It is helpful to draw a line from zero to a cross for the 'successful' score and then continue the line to end with a circle for the 'contented' score. Any differences of more than one are likely to be significant. However, it is up to you to place what significance you feel is appropriate within each total score and between each of the factor scores. Draw a line between all of your total scores so that you obtain a 'zigzag' graph. This helps you to see differences between scores.

Life balance chart

Balance											
0	Compromise		4	5	Contentment		8	9	Compensation		12
'R' Relationships at work											
0	1	2	3	4	5	6	7	8	9	10	11	12
'S' Status of the job											
0	1	2	3	4	5	6	7	8	9	10	11	12
'A' Authority at work											
0	1	2	3	4	5	6	7	8	9	10	11	12
'M' Material reward											
0	1	2	3	4	5	6	7	8	9	10	11	12
'N' Nature of the job											
0	1	2	3	4	5	6	7	8	9	10	11	12
'L' Leisure time											
0	1	2	3	4	5	6	7	8	9	10	11	12
'F' Family life											
0	1	2	3	4	5	6	7	8	9	10	11	12

Interpreting your life balance chart

The life balance chart shows where there is harmony, or lack of it, in seven key areas of your life. Generally, scores around the middle of the chart indicate that you are in harmony with these areas of your life.

Other words that are sometimes used in the same way as 'harmony' are 'life-adjustment', 'contentment' or 'balance'.

How content you are in any one of these seven areas of your life can change, depending upon the circumstances in which you find yourself and how you respond to them. You may decide deliberately to make changes yourself as a result of becoming aware of what is happening to you.

There are many external factors that can, and will, arise which threaten your life balance, but maintaining harmony within yourself is the best means of coping. To the Chinese Taoist sage, acknowledged as the ultimate example of a contented person, the main purpose in life, the ultimate goal, is to achieve and maintain a state of harmony.

If your scores on the life balance test are in the 'contentment' area, you have achieved this desirable, but elusive, state of 'balance' where conflict has been resolved.

If you ask yourself 'Am I happy?', listen deep within yourself as you answer. If you are not truly happy, you may have been deceiving yourself when you completed the questionnaire – subconsciously choosing responses that you somehow knew would help you avoid confronting areas of your life you would rather not be aware of.

Another possibility could be that, after you have examined critical areas of your life by means of the test, little things you had previously ignored have risen to the surface. They have become more distinct as you brought them into focus. As you become aware that they are more significant than you were previously prepared to admit, you realize that the harmony was only a pretence, so your life is again out of balance.

Alternatively, you may have already 'moved on'. That is, the process of taking the questionnaire and considering the issues it raises has led you to better understand areas of your life that could be improved or changed.

Human beings are restless. We constantly strive to get somewhere in our lives – mentally, physically, socially or spiritually. If we are successful in attaining our objectives, then we experience the contentment of someone who has 'arrived'. But this contentment is short-lived. Almost immediately, we want to get somewhere else or achieve something different.

The psychologist Will Schutz, whose ideas are embodied in this commentary, said that the search itself is a joyful experience, simply because we begin to use ourselves more fully as we realize our potential: 'As a human being, my ultimate aim is a joyful life. Joy is the feeling that results from using myself – my thinking and feeling capacities, my senses, my body, and my spirit – in all the ways I am capable. I am less happy when I am not using myself and when I am blocking myself' (*Profound Simplicity*, 1979). Consequently, the search for, and maintenance of, harmony is our life's work. If we tell ourselves we are content, without actually feeling in harmony, we are lying to ourselves and are not 'fully' alive.

Contentment

Look at those scores outside the zone of balance or 'contentment'. In these areas you will feel dissatisfied and may well experience conflicting emotions.

The life balance test is based upon the principle that we can change our lives if we wish to. The first step is awareness of the psychological territory in which we find ourselves.

Those problems that we feel will prevent us changing in the ways we would like are less difficult when we examine them in the light of awareness. When problems remain buried or suppressed they often assume a frightening size, out of all proportion to their real significance. It is this fear of them, rather than their reality, that makes us reluctant to tackle them head on.

The LBT presupposes that you have energy with which you attempt to achieve happiness. This is a dynamic process by which effort can shift, depending on what is important or difficult for you at different times in your life. When you achieve in one area, you may transfer your energy to another.

At the same time, because of difficulties or fears about one area, you may avoid it. When you achieve just the right balance in an area of your life, this becomes harmonious.

This is not to say that the situation then stays the same for ever, because it seems to be part of human nature that restlessness or a new expectation sets in, with the result that often constant attention and adjustment go on. Nothing is 'right' or 'wrong' about harmony. There is no external, regulatory or moral code that is able to say what harmony is or should be. Ultimately, it is you who feel, with body, mind and spirit, that you are achieving what you want.

Compromise

The reasons for your compromising in these areas may relate to one or more of the following, though it is good to add your own, making your situation clearer:

- You lack real opportunity in these areas.

- You have resigned or given up.

- You have taken a deliberate decision not to strive in these areas.

- You lack awareness of, or deny, how important they are.

- ....

- ....

Compensation

It is possible that your high-scoring areas are compensations for (or make up for) lack of achievement in areas represented by your low scores. These may be among the reasons you give yourself, but add your own, as these will make your situation clearer:

- I can't help it.

- It's expected of me.

- People regard or respect me this way.

- I have to do well in this way, as I cannot do other things so well.

- ....

- ....

Implications of your results

The implications are always unique to you because of your unique character, circumstances and experience. However, feelings, fears and motivations are common to everyone. Consequently some guidance, based upon this common experience, is possible.

It should be stressed that the following is for guidance only and you can choose to reject it if is not found helpful. Nothing in this is meant to be critical, and there is no intention to apportion blame in any way. All human beings are subject to self-deception. Therefore blaming is not helpful – though becoming aware always is!

The aim is to explain, to understand and to enable you to change if, with awareness, that is what you desire.

The first step of change is to gain awareness of the psychological territory in which you find yourself – in order to get to where you want to be, it is helpful to know where you are starting from!

Bear in mind that it's quite natural that a need to achieve in one area of your life can lead to a temporary neglect of others. Indeed, some lack of contentment may be necessary so that we can get things done – particularly things that are difficult and need a certain degree of single-mindedness. Difficulty arises only when an area of your life is neglected. This may be due to fear or lack of confidence – not realizing the effect that this may be having upon your life.

The results can therefore indicate areas of relative failure, the consequences of which, if ignored, can lead to conflict, compromise, rigid attitudes, maladaptive behaviour or even illness.

Now is the time to tackle issues that are disharmonious. Recognition that they exist implies that you have the energy and desire to deal with them. When you accomplish this, you complete the energy cycle. You feel liberated and more like your 'real' self. But if, out of fear, you bury them, your energy becomes locked. This does not do you, or anybody else, any good. Repressing energy usually leads to boredom, tiredness, illness, frustration, or anger with other people.

Awareness

Awareness of what is causing disharmony in our lives is the key that opens the way to our goal. It is only our own fear about changing that stops us getting there. When fear is overcome, we gain awareness of the futility of limiting ourselves and how much we can achieve.

Each one of us is two persons: the person we are now and the person we know we can be. The aim of each of us is to bring out the latter person and develop our self to the fullest.

Fears about change

Often we are afraid to try to be our 'real self' in case people reject us, laugh at us or even ignore us. It is usually such fears that hold us back. But if we do not try to actualize the person we want to be, we only have ourselves to blame. Too often, we make victims of ourselves by blaming others, pretending that it is they who are holding us back. That it is we who are holding ourselves back is the truth that is sometimes too uncomfortable for us to admit.

We can find many excuses for not becoming the person we know we can be. But this gets us nowhere. Eventually we become angry with ourselves for letting ourselves down. The easy way out is to blame others, saying that it is their fault, when the truth is that we are afraid to try.

Ultimately, there is only one way – do what you want to do; be the person you want to be, to your fullest. You will discover that other people like you best this way.

Successful versus contented

Whatever the total of your score, whether you find yourself overall in the area of compromise, contentment or compensation, it is worth asking why your sub-scores may not be the same. For example, to what extent does the fact that I am higher on a successful sub-score than a contented one imply that I am doing something that I am unhappy with? Does this unhappiness express itself in ways I do not like? Also, to what extent does the fact that I have a higher sub-score on contented than successful imply that I am unhappy by not doing something I would like to do more of? If this makes me feel suppressed, does this lead me to behave in ways I do not like?

Compensations versus compromises

You may already know that there are areas of your life that are compensating for what you have given up in other areas. Alternatively, you may deny, feel guilty about or not be aware of your true feelings in these areas. In other words, you may have feelings of conflict or guilt that you do not normally tell yourself about. It is possible that you could be pretending you are satisfied, though this has a hollow feeling, since at a deeper level you are not satisfied at all.

It is your high and low scores that require analysis, since they represent areas of your life that are probably out of balance.

Conflict

It is possible that your low scores represent sacrifices you are making in order to obtain more out of life in those areas represented by your higher scores, in your area of harmony. If so, are these sacrifices based on decisions that you have thought about clearly and honestly? Or do they have underlying emotional causes, which you may feel driven by and which you are not clear about? Denial of a factor in this area may represent hidden or suppressed emotions, indicating feelings of guilt or other conflict. Sometimes, paradoxically, the more vehemently people deny the importance of some aspect of their life, the deeper the conflict is buried in their subconscious.

Conflict arises when there is a split between a feeling and a thought. For example, people may feel a certain way, but think they should not have that feeling. They may not be able to resolve whether their feeling or behaviour is proper or correct, or whether it is silly. In particular, they may think that having such feelings will make others reject them.

For example, if a person feels resentful towards his or her children, the issue is not whether the children have in fact done something bad, but that the person, wanting to be a responsible parent, feels guilty about having such feelings. The usual way of trying to cope with such painful feelings is to blame the children, in this example, for the situation that caused those feelings.

Emotional consequences

Are you happy with the situation as it stands? Ask yourself how long these areas of compromise in your life can be left as they are. What are the consequences to you of being relatively unfulfilled in areas of your life that have, until now, remained relatively unexplored or neglected?

Rigidity

If you cannot resolve a conflict, you may try to forget it. You put it into your subconscious mind or bury it. But repressed feelings don't go away. The fact that you try not to be aware of them means that they can often affect, and influence, you in ways that are not obvious. For example, in order to cope with repressed conflict, you may, in common with most people, adopt a rigid attitude or type of behaviour.

Let us take a more concrete example of feeling guilty about not earning enough money. People in this situation may say that it is wrong for people to earn more money than them. They may produce logical arguments about the damaging effects of materialism. However, the opinion may be based, without awareness, ultimately upon a repressed feeling that is the opposite of the expressed one.

Defence mechanisms

You may also use defence mechanisms to cope with conflicts between feelings and thoughts. There are various defence mechanisms known to psychologists, who have terms for them such as 'projection' or displacement'. What these mean is that you see your own situation in other people, ascribing to others what you are actually feeling yourself. You may criticize others for your lack of opportunity, or see yourself as a victim of circumstances. You may believe that your achievement, or lack of it, in any area helps other people more than yourself. You may use others to compensate you for what you feel unable to achieve for yourself.

What defence mechanisms do is attempt to pass the guilt, fear, shame or embarrassment from ourselves on to others.

Fear

How aware are you of your feelings? It is possible for example that, if you say 'lack of opportunity' or 'not important to me', the truth is that subconsciously you do not make opportunities or that it really is important but you don't want to admit it. This can arise out of fear of what might happen if you choose to change. Therefore out of fear there is denial that the feeling exists.

It is frequently the case that people who lack confidence in their ability to achieve in an area of their life are encouraged to overcome their fears by practice – by small achievements, or even plunging in and doing what is most difficult for them. This latter 'make or break' technique can work, though there is a danger that, having made an attempt – perhaps timidly or half-heartedly, owing to fear of failure – the person won't try again.

Self-deception

An alternative way to deal with conflict, and overcome it, is to gain insight into how it arose in the first place. This is the analytical method. Such insight frequently comes when people challenge themselves by questioning what they are achieving by feeling, and behaving in, the way they do. Understanding your self-deceptions is the key with which you can unlock repressed conflicts and cope with them objectively.

To understand self-deception is to understand what you get out of behaving, and feeling, the way you do. Why might you be willing to compromise with a certain aspect of your life? Why might you say you cannot do something when other people are fully aware that you can? Perhaps you are unaware that you get attention this way, without ever having to take the risk of proving yourself.

This is a difficult thing to do, but try assuming that you derive some benefit, perhaps subconsciously, from denying this aspect of your life. What do you get out of holding back or not being fulfilled? It could well be that you make conscious, or subconscious, rationalizations about the benefits of continuing to feel, or behave, the way you do. We sometimes call this the 'negative gain', the 'false friend' or the 'quick fix', because the effort you make in trying to convince yourself gets you nowhere. The following are common examples of self-deception:

- People like me better when I don't get involved.

- I wouldn't want to be too pushy.

- Although I want to change, people like me the way I am.

- I will get my reward in the end.

- I get sympathy from others this way.

- I'm not expected to make too much effort.

The characteristic of self-deception is that it provides only a temporary relief or comfort. Often self-deceptions are maintained over many years and have a nagging aspect associated with them. They are never strong enough to deal with the fear or conflict, and cumulatively self-deceptions are an abyss that is never filled.

Relationships at work

This covers your level of satisfaction with important relationships at work, not at home. Consequently, it relates to your relationships with colleagues, subordinates, customers or superiors, not your relationships with family and friends.

Relationships compensation scores 9–12

You are more than satisfied with your achievements in this area. This is fine – unless you personally feel that you are making too much of an effort in maintaining relationships with others, or feel that by doing so there is a personal cost to you that you wish you did not have to meet.

The question to ask yourself is whether the energy and effort you expend on creating and maintaining working relationships are causing you to neglect other areas of your life. The importance that you give to relationships could be providing you with an excuse for neglecting, or not dealing with, some areas of your life in which you could be compromising, if these are indicated by your results on the LBT (Life Balance Test).

Some people may be very social, but still not be satisfied with their relationships – hence they may try still harder. On the other hand, others can be satisfied with their relationships without necessarily being described as 'social' by nature.

Think about your own situation for a moment. Does the importance you place on relationships arise out of fear – being afraid of what might happen if your working relationships were not maintained?

You may have your own feelings as to why you place so much emphasis upon your relationships at work. Think for a moment about what might be driving you to be this way.

It sometimes helps to think through your own feelings by hearing what other people have felt was the truer and deeper explanation for their own situation. The following are some of the fears and excuses that have arisen for others. Tick or mark the ones that are also true for you. Add your own, if you can.

- Other people won't leave me alone.

- I've got to find others; they won't find me.

- People will not think I'm important if I don't spend time with them.

- They need help to join in.

If you have any of your own, different reasons, write them in below:

. . . .

. . . .

Are you satisfied with the reasons you give yourself, or do they have a hollow ring to them?

Relationships compromise scores 0–4

As you responded to the LBT, were you thinking of certain key, meaningful relationships that are on your mind at the present time, or were you thinking of all your relationships? You feel that you are not achieving in this area of your life. You may tell yourself that you are – but are you telling yourself the truth?

Lack of achievement in this area can be due to many causes. You may have little or no opportunity to build or maintain relationships at work, or you may have deliberately decided that it is not important to you to do so. You may feel that achievement in other areas of your life adequately compensate for your not achieving in the area of relationships.

Alternatively, it may be that the area of relationships is one you would like to change, but you do not know how to go about doing so. It may be helpful to ask yourself why you prevent yourself from achieving in this area. Do you see some advantage in keeping relationships distant? Are you afraid of getting closer to people? The question to ask yourself is 'Why don't I change things to make them better?'

Assuming that you derive some benefit – consciously or subconsciously – from having relationships the way they are, what are you achieving by 'underachieving' in this area of your life?

You may have your own feelings about why you place so little emphasis upon relationships at work. Think for a moment about what might be driving you to be this way.

It sometimes helps to think through your own feelings by hearing what other people have felt was the truer and deeper explanation for their own situation. The following are some of the fears and excuses that have arisen for others:

- This way I don't have to bother.

- People will not have expectations of me.

- I have lots of more important things to do.

- People may not accept me.

- People prefer me to keep distant; they will invite me to join in if they want to.

- I should not impose myself.

- I might be ignored.

Can you add your own reasons to this list?

....

....

In what ways might some or all of the above be self-deceptions?

Status of the job

It is your own feelings about your status which count – not those of others, or society in general. People with 'status' are often regarded as important, as 'senior' or as being 'at the top'. In this context, 'status' refers to the level or position you feel gives you the significance you want.

Status compensation scores 9–12

You feel that you have more than achieved a position that is appropriate for you. Ask yourself 'Is it easy to maintain this position?' Do you need status and for your own reasons have to make an effort to maintain it – and the feelings of self-worth that go with it – so that there could, consequently, be less satisfaction in other areas of your life? Take time to review any areas of compromise shown in your results. Is there one, or more, of these that you tend to ignore, or leave out, as a result of having achieved the status you hold?

Is there a possibility that you might be paying undue attention to status? If so, could this be out of fear of what might happen if you lost it? You may, for example, feel that turning your attention to other areas of your life poses a threat. You therefore tell yourself that it's better to have status than risk losing it. This in turn gives you a legitimate excuse, or way out of the conflict you feel, since you try to tell yourself that it's not worth doing anything about this situation. You may have your own feelings about why you place so much emphasis upon the status of your work. Think for a moment about what might be driving you to be this way.

It sometimes helps to think through your own feelings by hearing what other people have felt was the truer and deeper explanation for their situation. The following are some of the fears and excuses that have arisen for others:

- If I was not important, people would take no notice of me.

- People would not be able to get along without me.

- People might pass me by or ignore me if I did not have my position.

- People need me to be where I am.

If you have your own reasons, add them to the list.

. . . .

. . . .

Status compromise scores 0–4

Status may simply not be important to you, or it could be that you are not achieving what you want in this area of your life. It is for you to decide. You might be telling yourself that you do not have the opportunity to achieve in this area, but at the same time you could be holding back. For example, you could lack confidence in this area, and be reluctant to try in case you fail. The possibility of failure could be giving you a ready-made excuse not to try!

You may feel that achievement in other areas of your life adequately compensates for your not achieving in the area of the status of the work you do.

You can gain insight into your hidden motives by asking yourself what you achieve by keeping things as they are, ie by not changing the situation so that your feelings of status are increased.

You may have your own feelings about why you place so little emphasis upon the status of your work. Think for a moment about what might be driving you to be this way.

It sometimes helps to think through your own feelings by hearing what other people have felt was the truer and deeper explanation for their own situation. The following are some of the fears and excuses that often arise. Tick the ones that apply to you and add any others of your own.

- People prefer me when I am modest.

- If I do not put myself forward, I will avoid being ignored.

- It is unfair if I put myself above others.

- I will pretend that status is not important to me.

- I will give someone else a chance.

....

....

Are you really satisfied with these reasons, or could you be deceiving yourself?

Authority at work

This covers your level of satisfaction with the opportunity your work gives you for doing things in your own way. This has two elements – firstly, the authority of self-reliance or self-determination and, secondly, the power or influence you have over others. Some people feel they have authority because there is no one controlling them, while others feel they have authority because they are seen to be leaders.

Authority compensation scores 9–12

You have the authority that you want, but do you make sacrifices in other areas of your life in order to be able to work in this way? How does your need to work in your own way affect your preparedness to compromise – specifically in any areas indicated in your test results?

Do you maintain your authority to some extent out of a fear of losing it? Could it be that the authority you have gives you a reason to avoid confronting other areas in your life you find difficult? Do some of the areas of compromise, as shown in your results, help you to answer this last question?

You may have your own feelings about why you emphasize the area of authority. Think for a moment about what might be driving you to be this way. It sometimes helps to think through your own feelings by hearing what other people have felt was the truer and deeper explanation for their own situation. The following are some of the fears and excuses that have arisen for others:

- I have to look after people; they cannot do it themselves.
- People ask me what they ought to do.
- I feel uncomfortable if I can't control what happens.
- People may not respect me if I'm not seen to be in charge.
- I am helping others by doing things my way.

Can you add your own reasons to this list?

. . . .

. . . .

Are these truly reasons, or is there some self-deception?

Authority compromise scores 0–4

Authority may really not be important to you; not having authority can give you a chance to concentrate on other areas of your life, such as any areas of compensation highlighted on your life balance chart.

Alternatively, it can mean that you want authority but do not have it at the moment. If this is the case, you must ask yourself why. Is it because you are afraid of taking it on, or are you afraid of directing others or directing your own life? Do you see taking on authority as a threat to you – consequently regarding it as something that is best avoided? Sometimes people avoid taking on authority over others because they imagine the humiliation they would feel if they lost the respect or control, or were seen as a failure. You may have your own feelings as to why you place so little emphasis upon authority at work. Think for a moment about what might be driving you to be this way.

It sometimes helps to think through your own feelings by hearing what other people have felt was the truer and deeper explanation for their own situation. The following are some of the fears and excuses that have arisen for others:

- I may not be appreciated if I take authority to do things my way.

- People may not let me.

- I'm not as capable as people think.

- I prefer people telling me what to do.

- I could look foolish.

- I'm not skilled or clever enough.

- If I haven't authority, I can't be blamed if things go wrong.

- This way, I never risk finding out whether I'm really capable of doing the things I pretend I could do.

Can you add your own reasons to this list?

....

....

How satisfied are you with the reasons you give yourself?

Material reward

This covers the level of satisfaction you obtain, materially, from work – that is, your income and other financial benefits by which you are rewarded for your services. There is nothing final, fair or absolute about the amount you receive, just your own feelings about how satisfactory this is to you at this time.

Material compensation scores 9–12

You are pleased with what you earn, which may even be more than you actually need. You may feel that you earn a disproportionate amount of money for what you do, or you may simply feel that your income is sufficient for your purposes.

Money can be a strong motivator or a weak one – usually the former. In your case, it seems that the pursuit of income has led you to pay less attention to areas of compromise indicated in your results. Which of the other areas of your life are you 'passing on' in order to achieve materially?

People often pursue money and make sacrifices in order to buy themselves the time, opportunity or materials to do what they want at some time in the future. Psychologists often call this 'delayed gratification'. Ask yourself if concentrating on one area of attainment (in this case material reward), and thus delaying attainment in other areas, is what you want.

You may have your own feelings about why you place so much emphasis upon material reward. Think for a moment about what might be driving you to be this way.

It sometimes helps to think through your own feelings by hearing what other people have felt was the truer and deeper explanation for their own situation. The following are some of the fears and excuses that have arisen for others:

- I don't ask people to pay me as much as they do.

- The money I earn is for others, not for me.

- People expect it of me.

- It just goes with the job.

Can you add your own reasons to this list?

. . . .

. . . .

How do you justify any of the above?

Material compromise scores 0–4

Money is not important to you, or you pretend it is not, or you are not achieving the level of income you feel you should. If the latter is true, could it be that you have consciously given up on money because it is more worthwhile to achieve in other areas of life? Examine any areas of compensation in your results and see if this could be the case.

If you really are discontented with this area of your life and are compromising on this factor, ask yourself 'Why?' and 'What am I gaining?' Does the situation arise out of fear of trying to achieve in this area of your life?

You may have your own feelings about why you place so little emphasis upon material reward. Think for a moment about what might be driving you to be this way.

It sometimes helps to think through your own feelings by hearing what other people have felt was the truer and deeper explanation for their own situation. The following are some of the fears and excuses that have arisen for others:

- I don't want to be seen as someone motivated by money.

- Money embarrasses me.

- I would look ridiculous if I tried to earn money and failed.

- I could earn more, but people want me to spend my time with them.

- People wouldn't like me if I earned more money.

- People who earn money haven't a heart.

- I'll let others decide if I am worth more than I'm being paid.

Can you add your own reasons to this list?

....

....

Are you satisfied with the reasons you give yourself, or do they have a hollow ring? If so, you may be becoming aware of ways in which you could be deceiving yourself. Overcoming self-deception is the aim of this exercise!

Nature of the job

This covers the level of satisfaction you obtain from the nature of the work you do. It is concerned with the job function and what you achieve in its performance – irrespective of the people you meet, the authority your job may have, or the money you are paid for doing it.

Nature of the job compensation scores 9–12

You appear satisfied with your work. In order to do it, you may even be prepared to lose out on some areas of your life. These will appear in your test results.

Are you compromising in any of those areas because of the larger effort you put into actually doing your job?

You see your job as being worthwhile, but this could also be an excuse for not achieving in other areas of your life in which you may be compromising. You may have your own feelings about why you place so much emphasis upon the nature of the work you do. Think for a moment about what might be driving you to be this way.

It sometimes helps to think through your own feelings by hearing what other people have felt was the truer and deeper explanation for their own situation. The following are some of the fears and excuses that have arisen for others:

- I have to do this job because no one else would.

- I am helping people who can't help themselves.

- I don't have to stretch myself too far.

- People are happy if I'm happy in my work.

- I am prepared to make a sacrifice for others.

Can you add your own reasons to this list?

....

....

Are you satisfied with the reasons you give yourself?

Nature of the job compromise scores 0–4

You are not satisfied with the essential nature of your work. It could be that you are not doing what you would really like to do. Do you put up with this situation because you feel that you are achieving in other areas of your life? In that case, you should look specifically at the compensation areas of your life balance chart.

Are you afraid that, by changing the nature of your work, you will affect the balance you have in these areas? If so, this gives you a ready-made excuse for not changing your job and putting the blame on others.

Are you delaying, putting off or avoiding doing what you want to do? Do you feel that there are pressures upon you that you can't avoid, preventing you from fulfilling yourself in this area? You could be imagining that others are expecting you to 'stick with it' and may be using them as an excuse for not changing. You should ask yourself whether you are attributing feelings to other people that they do not really have.

You may have your own feelings about why you place so little emphasis upon the nature of the work you do. Think for a moment about what might be driving you to be this way.

It sometimes helps to think through your own feelings by hearing what other people have felt was the truer and deeper explanation for their own situation. The following are some of the fears and excuses that have arisen for others:

- What I do doesn't really matter.
- I'll get what I want eventually.
- I like to make sacrifices for others.
- It is good to be selfless.
- It is better to do what others want me to do.
- It is too late to change.

Can you add your own reasons to this list?

. . . .

. . . .

Are you satisfied with the reasons you give yourself?

Leisure time

This covers the level of satisfaction you obtain from your leisure time achievements. These can include hobbies, sport and other activities or interests that are not work related and are not immediately connected with your family. Leisure time is concerned with the area of your private time.

Leisure compensation scores 9–12

What you achieve in your leisure time is highly important to you. You may feel more successful with your leisure activities than you do with some other areas of your life in which you might be compromising. Lack of achievement in these areas can be due to lack of opportunity, motivation or success, and may lead you to make your leisure activities a compensation.

Ask yourself if your leisure time achievements are being used as a way of avoiding, or denying, the importance of these other areas of your life. This could be out of fear of confronting them head on. You may, for example, feel unable to achieve the authority or the position you want, but tell yourself that this is not really important to you.

One way of telling whether these other areas really are important to you is to ask yourself 'Am I critical of others who achieve in these areas?' This type of searching will indicate if you repress, or deny, the conflicts you have.

For you, leisure is perhaps an area in which you feel highly satisfied and want to put still more effort into. Alternatively, it may be an area of life that you use to compensate for other areas that you have fears about changing.

You may have your own feelings as to why you place so much emphasis upon your leisure time activities. Think for a moment about what might be driving you to be this way.

It sometimes helps to think through your own feelings by hearing what other people have felt was the truer and deeper explanation for their own situation. The following are some of the fears and excuses that have arisen for others:

- People should do more for others.

- It is good to be selfless.

- Success in the material world means nothing to me.

- I never had the opportunity that others had.

Can you add your own reasons to this list?

· ·

· ·

Are these truly reasons, or are they merely excuses for behaving in this way?

Leisure compromise scores 0–4

It could be that you have decided not to achieve in this area of life because it is less important to you than others that rate more highly. It could also be the case that leisure time is the one area that, owing to other pressures of life, people give up first, since it has the least to do with survival in the modern world. A relaxing spare-time, or a hectic leisure time, pursuit can be all-absorbing and time-consuming, or it can have little meaning in a person's life.

It is often the case that people neglect this area, feeling that they will apportion more time to it later on when they have the opportunity to do so, even putting it off until they retire from work. Alternatively, leisure may be an area that you would like to be more important in your life. You may have failed to pursue leisure-related opportunities in the past, for one reason or another. You may have your own feelings as to why you currently place so little emphasis upon leisure time. Think for a moment about what might be driving you to be this way.

It sometimes helps to think through your own feelings by hearing what other people have felt was the truer and deeper explanation for their own situation. The following are some of the fears and excuses that have arisen for others:

- Other things must come first.
- I will not be seen as an achiever.
- I have no time.
- People don't expect me to spend time in this area; I'd be letting them down if I did.
- Other people won't let me do what I want.
- I'd look foolish.

Can you add your own reasons to this list?

....

....

How many of the above are at least partly self-deceptions?

Family life

This covers the level of satisfaction you obtain from your family life. Family, in this sense, means those people closest to you – relatives, or people who, for emotional or legal reasons, can be considered to be relatives.

Family life compensation scores 9–12

You feel achievement in this area of your life. You may like your life to be this way. But pause to consider if it could be compensating you for lack of achievement in other areas of your life suggested by any scores in the area of compromise. See whether your family life makes up for what you are lacking in one or more of these areas.

It is, of course, possible to be satisfied with family life, paradoxi-cally, because you have no family and don't want any – though it is unlikely that your score is high for this reason. It is most likely to be because you have a family and the strong importance this has for you.

It is nonetheless worth asking yourself whether the effort you spend on this area of your life prevents you from achieving in other areas. If you are entirely assured in family life, does this give you a convenient excuse for not trying to achieve in other areas? Such areas of your life may well present more of a threat to you than you make out.

You may have your own feelings as to why you place so much emphasis upon family life. Think for a moment about what might be driving you to be this way.

It sometimes helps to think through your own feelings by hearing what other people have felt was the truer and deeper explanation for their own situation. The following are some of the fears and excuses that have arisen for others:

- If I attend properly to my family, I won't have time for anything else.

- My family can't manage without me.

- If I am needed outside of my family, people will let me know.

- I think that other people have wrong values.

- I no longer have the skills or abilities.

- My family cannot manage without me.

- It is my duty to look after my family.

Can you add your own reasons to this list?

. . . .

. . . .

Do they have a hollow ring to them? How many are there because of self-deception?

Family life compromise scores 0–4

It is possible that your low score on this factor indicates that you do not have a family life or that it is not an important area for you. But it could mean that other areas of life are affecting your opportunity to find fulfilment within your family. If this is the case, you might be compromising family life in order to find gratification in other areas of your life, perhaps trading off achievement in one or more of the areas of compensation and thereby denying the area of family life.

You may see this as a necessary, temporary feature. For example, people sometimes say that they will not get married until they have earned enough money or achieved a position that will enable them to support a family.

Denying satisfaction in the area of family could suggest conflict. This could be out of fear of exposing oneself to rejection, emotional entanglements or dependence on others. Close involvements can seem frightening.

You may have your own feelings as to why you place so little emphasis upon family life. Think for a moment about what might be driving you to be this way.

It sometimes helps to think through your own feelings by hearing what other people have felt was the truer and deeper explanation for their own situation. The following are some of the fears and excuses that have arisen for others:

- I couldn't cope with a family.

- I wouldn't be wanted.

- I am not attractive enough.

- I don't need a family.

- I make up for it by providing for or helping other people in other ways.

- I'm a failure as a family member.

- Nobody is attractive to me.

- They have got to stand on their own feet.

Can you add your own reasons to this list?

. . . .

. . . .

How many are genuine and how many self-deception? What fears lead you to do this? Remember that overcoming self-deception is the aim of this exercise!

Life balance development exercises

Section 1: where am I now?

The pursuit of a balanced life – of harmony – is a never-ending quest; our ambitions, interests and needs are forever changing. They are dynamic.

For some the degree of imbalance is more constant and more severe than for others, possibly because basic areas of compromise in life have, for one reason or another, never been tackled. Indeed, often the situation gradually gets worse as we over-compensate for these areas of relative failure. But, even for those who currently enjoy a balanced life, the very dynamism of both internal and external factors means that this state of relative harmony may be fleeting or temporary.

Your life balance analysis, therefore, has provided only a snap-shot of where you are now. Whether you currently have several areas of compromise and compensation or whether you are in harmony, the situation can and probably will change.

With this dynamic reality in mind, the exercises have been designed not only to help take you from where you are now to where you want to be, but once there to help you control your own life in such a way that you feel both successful and contented – even if your ambition drives you toward more of both!

Because the life balance test is built upon this fundamental principle of continuous change, it can be used periodically to monitor your progress towards your vision of a more successful and contented life. This book is simply to help you steer the route towards that goal.

No more financial worries

Imagine that you have just been informed that you have been left an income for life. It may be in the will of a near or distant relative, a friend or someone you met only once – whichever is the most realistic possibility for you.

Unfortunately, there is no gigantic lump sum! You have not become a multimillionaire with money to spend as and when you wish. Instead, you will receive just enough to remove any existing or potential financial problems that you may have and to ensure that the lifestyle you currently enjoy or strive to maintain is guaranteed – for life. Sufficient finance will be provided to pay off any current debts, replace your car(s) and when necessary maintain your house, buy your food and even fund your annual holidays.

Sit back. Relax and imagine yourself in this situation: no more financial worries. When you feel that you have captured the mood, allow yourself to experience it for 5 or 10 minutes, mentally wandering through the implications of your new-found situation. Think about the areas of your life that may be affected: your job, your home life, your hobbies, your daily routine.

You may feel that nothing will change. You may already enjoy sufficient guaranteed financial security, so that this makes no real difference. That is fine. On the other hand you may currently be financially secure but strive to make yourself 'more and more secure' as an insurance against illness or redundancy. Worse still, you may not feel at all financially secure – until now! Whatever your personal situation, think about these new circumstances in which you find yourself.

Before you lose the images that you have recently conjured, look at Exercise 1. The seven major areas of your life are listed column 1. Consider any changes or differences that you make in these areas, and write them in column 2. Example possible changes to summarize in column 2 would be: Nature – 'Work less overtime'; Family life – 'Spend more time Leisure time – 'Take up golf again'; and so on.

Record in column 3 the direction of this change. The the change is a plus (+) for an area that is currently compromise and a minus (−) for an area that is currently of compensation.

It is, of course, possible to be satisfied with family life, paradoxically, because you have no family and don't want any – though it is unlikely that your score is high for this reason. It is most likely to be because you have a family and the strong importance this has for you.

It is nonetheless worth asking yourself whether the effort you spend on this area of your life prevents you from achieving in other areas. If you are entirely assured in family life, does this give you a convenient excuse for not trying to achieve in other areas? Such areas of your life may well present more of a threat to you than you make out.

You may have your own feelings as to why you place so much emphasis upon family life. Think for a moment about what might be driving you to be this way.

It sometimes helps to think through your own feelings by hearing what other people have felt was the truer and deeper explanation for their own situation. The following are some of the fears and excuses that have arisen for others:

- If I attend properly to my family, I won't have time for anything else.

- My family can't manage without me.

- If I am needed outside of my family, people will let me know.

- I think that other people have wrong values.

- I no longer have the skills or abilities.

- My family cannot manage without me.

- It is my duty to look after my family.

Can you add your own reasons to this list?

. . . .

. . . .

Do they have a hollow ring to them? How many are there because of self-deception?

Family life compromise scores 0–4

It is possible that your low score on this factor indicates that you do not have a family life or that it is not an important area for you. But it could mean that other areas of life are affecting your opportunity to find fulfilment within your family. If this is the case, you might be compromising family life in order to find gratification in other areas of your life, perhaps trading off achievement in one or more of the areas of compensation and thereby denying the area of family life.

You may see this as a necessary, temporary feature. For example, people sometimes say that they will not get married until they have earned enough money or achieved a position that will enable them to support a family.

Denying satisfaction in the area of family could suggest conflict. This could be out of fear of exposing oneself to rejection, emotional entanglements or dependence on others. Close involvements can seem frightening.

You may have your own feelings as to why you place so little emphasis upon family life. Think for a moment about what might be driving you to be this way.

It sometimes helps to think through your own feelings by hearing what other people have felt was the truer and deeper explanation for their own situation. The following are some of the fears and excuses that have arisen for others:

- I couldn't cope with a family.

- I wouldn't be wanted.

- I am not attractive enough.

- I don't need a family.

- I make up for it by providing for or helping other people in other ways.

- I'm a failure as a family member.

- Nobody is attractive to me.

- They have got to stand on their own feet.

Can you add your own reasons to this list?

....

....

How many are genuine and how many self-deception? What fears lead you to do this? Remember that overcoming self-deception is the aim of this exercise!

Life balance development exercises

Section 1: where am I now?

The pursuit of a balanced life – of harmony – is a never-ending quest; our ambitions, interests and needs are forever changing. They are dynamic.

For some the degree of imbalance is more constant and more severe than for others, possibly because basic areas of compromise in life have, for one reason or another, never been tackled. Indeed, often the situation gradually gets worse as we overcompensate for these areas of relative failure. But, even for those who currently enjoy a balanced life, the very dynamism of both internal and external factors means that this state of relative harmony may be fleeting or temporary.

Your life balance analysis, therefore, has provided only a snapshot of where you are now. Whether you currently have several areas of compromise and compensation or whether you are in harmony, the situation can and probably will change.

With this dynamic reality in mind, the exercises have been designed not only to help take you from where you are now to where you want to be, but once there to help you control your own life in such a way that you feel both successful and contented – even if your ambition drives you toward more of both!

Because the life balance test is built upon this fundamental principle of continuous change, it can be used periodically to monitor your progress towards your vision of a more successful and contented life. This book is simply to help you steer the route towards that goal.

No more financial worries

Imagine that you have just been informed that you have been left an income for life. It may be in the will of a near or distant relative, a friend or someone you met only once – whichever is the most realistic possibility for you.

Unfortunately, there is no gigantic lump sum! You have not become a multimillionaire with money to spend as and when you wish. Instead, you will receive just enough to remove any existing or potential financial problems that you may have and to ensure that the lifestyle you currently enjoy or strive to maintain is guaranteed – for life. Sufficient finance will be provided to pay off any current debts, replace your car(s) and when necessary maintain your house, buy your food and even fund your annual holidays.

Sit back. Relax and imagine yourself in this situation: no more financial worries. When you feel that you have captured the mood, allow yourself to experience it for 5 or 10 minutes, mentally wandering through the implications of your new-found situation. Think about the areas of your life that may be affected: your job, your home life, your hobbies, your daily routine.

You may feel that nothing will change. You may already enjoy sufficient guaranteed financial security, so that this makes no real difference. That is fine. On the other hand you may currently be financially secure but strive to make yourself 'more and more secure' as an insurance against illness or redundancy. Worse still, you may not feel at all financially secure – until now! Whatever your personal situation, think about these new circumstances in which you find yourself.

Before you lose the images that you have recently conjured up, look at Exercise 1. The seven major areas of your life are listed in column 1. Consider any changes or differences that you would make in these areas, and write them in column 2. Examples of possible changes to summarize in column 2 would be: Nature of job – 'Work less overtime'; Family life – 'Spend more time at home'; Leisure time – 'Take up golf again'; and so on.

Record in column 3 the direction of this change. The direction of the change is a plus (+) for an area that is currently in the zone of compromise and a minus (−) for an area that is currently in the zone of compensation.

When completing this exercise you may find it helpful to recall the most meaningful learning you obtained from your reading of the life balance test analysis in relation to each of the seven major areas.

> Note: If you have already completed the exercises in Chapter 1 and/or
> Chapter 2, this would be a good time to review your findings in those areas
> and to take them into account in completing each of the following exercises.

Exercise 1

Area	Possible change	Amount of effort/time (+ or −)
Relationships at work		
Status		
Authority		
Material reward		
Nature of job		
Leisure time		
Family life		

Soon – no more worries at all

In the same way as you had to 'get into' the situation described in Exercise 1, you now have to visualize a completely different set of circumstances. Once again you will need solitude and time.

The situation this time is that you are terminally ill. You have recently been informed by your doctor that, although you will be able to function normally and give an outward appearance of excellent health for at least another two to three years, your life expectancy cannot extend much beyond that period.

First, try to picture or listen to yourself receiving the news. You decide the type of illness – whatever feels right. Once you have absorbed the news, begin to focus on the differences that this will make to your life. Think about the changes that you may need to make.

Fortunately, you have plenty of time to make meaningful changes. You don't need to rush around finalizing wills, insurance and the like – all of that can be sorted out in a couple of weeks. Focus on the major areas of your life – your career, your family, your leisure pursuits and your time. Work through each of these in terms of any adjustments or rebalancing. Will you spend more or less time on certain areas? Contemplate your new circumstances for however long feels comfortable.

Now, just as you did in Exercise 1, list any changes or differences that you may now decide to make in these major areas of your life. Examples would include identical ones to those given for Exercise 1. Others might be 'Forget status', 'Transfer authority' and so on.

Exercise 2

Area	Possible change	Amount of effort/time (+ or −)
Relationships at work		
Status		
Authority		
Material reward		
Nature of job		
Leisure time		
Family life		

No fear of flying

By now you know how to set the scene for your imaging exercises, so we won't go through that again. This time around you have no unnatural fears. Of course, you may still run (or fight) if someone chases you with a hatchet, but your day-to-day worries and anxieties have gone. Things that have already happened are over and done with – not worth worrying about. Things that have not yet happened are in the future – so why feel anxious now?

What sort of things used to cause these daily concerns and anxieties? Maybe it was a feeling that you were not up to a task with which you had been charged? Forget it, because in your new self you are extremely competent – and confident enough to know it. Possibly others – relatives, friends, colleagues – may not like you if you behave in certain ways. Again, forget it – this new you doesn't worry about what others think. You know that, because you are now the self you want to be, you like yourself. And, because you like yourself, others like you too!

Maybe you feel that others don't rate you as important. Well, you are. You are a significant individual making a significant contribution. You know that. Submerse yourself in this fearless, well-adjusted, competent, confident image. Allow yourself to feel good. You are capable of accomplishing anything you turn your hand to – potential unlimited!

This time, when completing the now familiar table below, you may come up with goals and targets in your career, in your leisure pursuits and in your home and family life that surpass your previous ambitions.

> Note: The following exercise should be a particularly useful one in which to reconsider any desired changes in your day-to-day behaviour patterns arising from your findings from the exercises in Chapter 1 and in your career ambitions and plans arising from your findings from completing the exercises in Chapter 2.

Exercise 3

Area	Possible change	Amount of effort/time (+ or −)
Relationships at work		
Status		
Authority		
Material reward		
Nature of job		
Leisure time		
Family life		

Section 2: 'MISELF' (my ideal self)

In Section 1 of the life balance development exercises you examined yourself in three different and hypothetical situations. From each of these three different angles you reviewed the seven major areas of your life, noting ways in which you might want to change the balance to suit your changed circumstances. The important questions are:

- Which of these changes should you be making anyway – right now?

- Is your need for financial security real or perceived?

- Are your fears limiting your new potential?

You will address these issues in this section.

To prepare yourself to create a 'MISELF' template you should return to your life balance test analysis and reconsider its findings in the light of the outputs from the exercises in Section 1, along with the findings from the previous chapters. In particular, focus on the following:

1 Your scores for 'successful' and 'contented'. Would the spread of scores be markedly different if they were based on your 'ideal self' (ie a self that felt secure and was free from irrational fear)? If so, in which areas and by how much?

2 Areas of compromise. Are you better able to understand your reasons for compromising – possibly underachieving – in these areas of your life? Reread the suggested possibilities that are listed in the analysis. After you have considered these points, reread the specific section on each of your areas of compromise. Try to address honestly the possible fears and excuses that are given as examples or you have revealed to yourself.

3 Areas of compensation. Can you better understand why you are compensating, possibly overachieving – in these areas? Again, consider the examples given in the narrative on each specific area of compensation. Do any of these, or others, apply to you?

Creating a 'MISELF' template

In Exercise 4 you can compare 'how you are' and 'how you want to be' by drawing from the results of all of your work so far.

Consider each of the seven major areas in turn. In column 2 use single words or short phrases to summarize your present state, situation or feeling about that area. In column 3, use words to describe how you want to be. Whether you use simple adjectives, nouns or action phrases doesn't really matter. The main point is that you recognize your current self in column 2 and your ideal self in column 3.

Exercise 4

1 Area	2 Present self	3 'MISELF'
Relationships at work		
Status		
Authority		
Material reward		
Nature of job		
Leisure time		
Family life		

Section 3: an action plan for change

You now have an image of how you would like to be. It is time to set about turning that into action and a practical reality.

The first step is to define some concrete objectives.

Objectives

It may be that you have already phrased your entries in column 3 of Exercise 4 as objectives. It is more likely that they are presently a little cloudier than that. An objective should be tangible and quantifiable. It must be capable of being measured. It is also important to set timescales in which to achieve objectives. This scientific approach helps to focus the mind towards the attainment of required results and can also help to clarify the objective itself.

For example, if your entry against 'Relationships at work' in column 3 of Exercise 4 was 'Build stronger relationships with colleagues at work', you could on the face of it use that statement as your objective as well. But is it quantifiable? Can it be measured? By when will it be achieved?

The statement obviously needs some work if it is to become meaningful, practicable and objective. So how do you go about converting this statement into a meaningful objective? The two key words are 'What?' and 'How?'

If you ask yourself 'What will be different when I have achieved this aim?', you begin to visualize the measures that then lead you back towards quantifying the objective itself. In this case you may know that you have achieved it when colleagues begin to demand more of your time, to seek your advice, to share their problems with you and so on. This becomes your measure of success.

If you then ask yourself 'How will I go about achieving it?', you begin to think about which colleagues you wish or need to work on. Are they in your own department or function or in another? Are they peers, subordinates or superiors? And what do you need to do to strengthen relationships? Be more proactive? Make a point of popping into people's offices frequently? Suggest ways in which your section can help them? Hold regular meetings?

You now have a basis on which to quantify and measure your objectives. You should also be able to work out a timescale based on your feel for how long it will take to 'convert' the required number of colleagues to your new interpersonal behaviour.

Thus, in this example, you might end up with something along the following lines:

Objective	To strengthen interpersonal relationships with key staff in the finance department so that we work more closely together in future.
Process(es)	1. Daily chat re problems.
	2. Provide regular management information to them.
	3. Hold joint meetings once per month.
Measure(s)	1. Finance invite me to their meetings.
	2. Finance staff members ask for my advice.
	3. We begin to work as a team.
Timescale	6 months

My action plan

In Exercise 5 your task will be to work on each of the areas where you intend to make some changes – those where 'MISELF' differed from 'my present self' in Exercise 4.

Remember that deciding an objective is of little use unless you think through and then implement the process changes to achieve it. These may be as simple as, for example:

- 'Leave my briefcase in the office on Friday evenings.'

- 'Leave the office promptly at 5.30 each evening' in the case of leisure time or family-related objectives.

- 'Apply for every vacancy I see for a [type of job]' in the case of objectives related to the nature of the job.

On this latter point, if you find that a number of your desired areas of change are related to your existing career circumstances it may be worth looking back at your results in Chapter 2 before finalizing your action plan.

It is also important to note that completion of your action plan is no 'one-minute solution'. You are dealing with your life adjustment – the very essence of your being – and, consequently, you will need to apply serious thought and endeavour to required areas of change.

Whatever route you choose, it is unlikely to be a 'piece of cake'!

Exercise 5

Area	Objectives	Processes involved	Measures of success	By when? (date)
Relationships at work				
Status				
Authority				
Material reward				
Nature of job				
Leisure time				
Family life				

Section 4: monitoring and review

Theoretically this stage could go on for ever. Because of the dynamic nature of individuals, which we have explored throughout this book and particularly in these last exercises, life consists of continual adjustments and changes, even to 'maintain a straight line', in the same way that we continuously adjust the steering wheel on our car, even on a long straight road. Therefore we could reapply the life balance process immediately upon completing it! In practice this should not be necessary, as once we have learnt how to use the tools to discover harmony we will instinctively feel the need to readjust when any area is slipping out of balance, in the same way as we instinctively adjust the steering wheel.

However, after working through your action plan, however long this takes, it would certainly be worth completing the life balance test at least one more time to note any changes in your profile.

Another simple measure to evaluate your progress is to ask those close to you – family, friends, colleagues – if they have noticed any changes.

The best test of all is to ask yourself, and give an honest, aware reply!

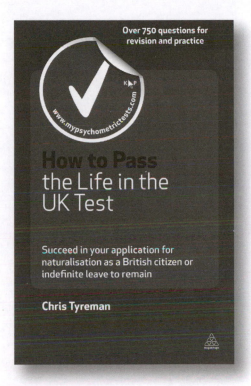

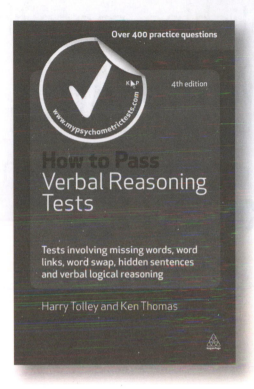

With over 42 years of
publishing, more than
80 million people

have succeeded in
business with thanks
to **Kogan Page**

www.

Page